Pro CSS3 Animation

Dudley Storey

Apress·

Pro CSS3 Animation

ISBN-13 (pbk): 978-1-4302-4722-7

ISBN-13 (electronic): 978-1-4302-4723-4

President and Publisher: Paul Manning
Lead Editor: Louise Corrigan
Technical Reviewer: Sylvain Galineau
Editorial Board: Steve Anglin, Ewan Buckingham, Gary Cornell, Louise Corrigan, Morgan Ertel, Jonathan Gennick, Jonathan Hassell, Robert Hutchinson, Michelle Lowman, James Markham, Matthew Moodie, Jeff Olson, Jeffrey Pepper, Douglas Pundick, Ben Renow-Clarke, Dominic Shakeshaft, Gwenan Spearing, Matt Wade, Tom Welsh
Coordinating Editor: Kevin Shea
Copy Editor: Elizabeth Berry
Compositor: SPi Global
Indexer: SPi Global
Artist: SPi Global
Cover Designer: Anna Ishchenko

Distributed to the book trade worldwide by Springer Science+Business Media New York, 233 Spring Street, 6th Floor, New York, NY 10013. Phone 1-800-SPRINGER, fax (201) 348-4505, e-mail orders-ny@springer-sbm.com, or visit www.springeronline.com.

For information on translations, please e-mail rights@apress.com, or visit www.apress.com.

Apress and friends of ED books may be purchased in bulk for academic, corporate, or promotional use. eBook versions and licenses are also available for most titles. For more information, reference our Special Bulk Sales–eBook Licensing web page at www.apress.com/bulk-sales.

Any source code or other supplementary materials referenced by the author in this text is available to readers at www.apress.com. For detailed information about how to locate your book's source code, go to www.apress.com/source-code.

To my grandparents, who never had the chance to read their grandson's first book.

—Dudley Storey

Contents at a Glance

Contents

About the Author

Photograph by Damain Blunt
(www.damianblunt.ca)

Dudley Storey has worked in digital design from the moment his parents bought him his first computer, a Commodore 64 with 16 colors and 64K of memory. Born in New Zealand, he graduated from the University of Auckland with degrees in Art History and Psychology. While continuing to work on more powerful computers, he created digital visualizations, programmable simulations, learning tools, and animations for the manufacturing industry, advertising, and architects. At the age of 28 he moved to Canada and began to teach multimedia at a series of institutions, gaining an increasing specialization in web technologies. While continuing to freelance, he has spent the last decade as an instructor in the New Media Production and Design course at SAIT Polytechnic in southern Alberta.

Four years ago, Dudley started a web development blog, www.demosthenes.info. Originally intended as a learning aid for his students, the site quickly gained wider attention. Encouraged by questions in his classes, the blog became a center for CSS experimentation and discussion.

An enthustiastic contributor to the web development community, Dudley has written for Smashing Magazine, A Student's Guide to Web Design, and other sites.

Dudley maintains an active Twitter presence (@dudleystorey) and participates in web design and development conferences around the world, including participation in the W3C Web Education Community Group.

When not lecturing, coding, or writing, Dudley enjoys cycling (especially long-distance self-supported bike tours), reading, and film.

Introduction

Welcome to Pro CSS3 Animation. This book teaches you how to use the full power of CSS to bring your web content to life with interactivity and a fresh visual approach. In the chapters that follow, you'll learn how to use cutting-edge industry standards to increase the visual appeal, accessibility, and popularity of your site.

Who This Book Is For

This book is designed for designers and coders with at least a few years of experience in web development who wish to rapidly upgrade their skills to the new W3C standards, or who desire to take their explorations of CSS Transforms, Transitions, and Animations in bold new directions. It is *not* an introductory web design text: the book assumes at least a basic understanding of HTML, CSS, and JavaScript. As web development is a multidisciplinary process, I'll also be addressing issues such as accessibility and semantics, concepts that the reader should be familiar with.

How This Book Is Structured

I've split the book into ten chapters. The first chapters introduce the fundamental components of CSS animation, while later chapters integrate animation with other web technologies.

Chapter 1 introduces CSS3, detailing its syntax and development and contrasting it with previous technologies.

Chapter 2 covers CSS3 Transforms and Transitions.

Chapter 3 shows how to use CSS3 Transitions with images, including gallery effects.

Chapter 4 integrates transitions with site user interaction elements such as buttons and menus.

Chapter 5 introduces the CSS Animation module.

Chapter 6 uses CSS3 Animations on all kinds of web content.

Chapter 7 shows how to integrate CSS3 Transitions and Animations with Scalable Vector Graphics (SVG) and CSS Filters.

Chapter 8 brings responsive web design and JavaScript together with CSS Animations.

Chapter 9 takes Transforms, Transitions, and Animations into the third dimension.

Chapter 10 looks to the future of web standards for visual effects and the various tools that can be used to streamline CSS web animation today.

Downloading the Code

The code for the examples shown in this book is available on the Apress web site, `www.apress.com`. A link can be found on the book's information page under the Source Code/Downloads tab. This tab is located underneath the Related Titles section of the page.

Contacting the Author

Should you have any questions or comments—or even spot a mistake you think I should know about—please feel free to contact me via e-mail (`dudley.storey@gmail.com`) or Twitter (`@dudleystorey`). I welcome your thoughts and feedback.

CHAPTER 1

■ ■ ■

CSS3 Fundamentals

For nearly two decades the Cascading Style Sheets (CSS) standard has been used to control the presentation of web pages. HTML defines what something *is:* a heading, a paragraph, an address, an image, etc. CSS describes how that element is *presented* to the user, including such qualities as its color, border, and dimensions. CSS includes presentational controls that few web designers even consider, such as the way text-to-speech services pronounce web page content.

All of the original presentational rules of CSS were designed for *static* content; that is, HTML elements that did not change over time. Until recently, if you wanted an image to fade in on a web page, there were only a few web technologies that you could use, the most popular of which were JavaScript and Flash. These technologies are not complete solutions, however; they have several serious disadvantages, as I'll discuss at the end of the chapter.

Now, we have the CSS3 Transforms, Transitions, and Animation Modules. These are extensions of CSS syntax that are supported in all modern browsers, overlapping, and in some cases, replacing the traditional roles of JavaScript and Flash. While CSS3 is not without its limitations, the technology is the way forward for a lot of dynamic web content.

To understand how we got here, you need to know where we've been. This introductory chapter will provide an overview of the CSS development process and where web development stands now, looking into the future.

Development of CSS

The independent evolution of web technologies has had something of a spotty history: browser vendors have sometimes propelled technology forward, while other technological implementations have complicated web development by adopting incompatible approaches.

The World Wide Web Consortium (W3C) was formed in an effort to try to synthesize and standardize web technologies into a series of specifications that were broadly supported by the web development industry. The W3C might be called the United Nations of web development: as an independent standards body, it can evaluate different proposals; create forums for discussions between industry, academia, developers, and other interests; negotiate and settle disagreements; and hammer out final specifications that everyone can agree to follow.

The CSS standard was developed by the CSS Working Group (CSSWG), a subgroup within the W3C. Over time, the CSSWG extended CSS to provide greater control over more aspects of web page content. As CSS 2.1 approached its final, finished status, further development of the specification was broken into multiple modules. Many of these modules started as "Level-3" proposals, leading developers to use the catch-all term *CSS3* for anything that followed CSS2.1. Technically, the web technologies that I focus on in this book—Animations, Transforms, and Transitions—are completely new Level-1 specifications, as they have no precedent in CSS1 or CSS2. Outside of very formal discussions, the web development industry refers to them collectively as *CSS3*, and I will continue to do so in this book.

At the same time, browser developers continued to innovate. Many of the CSS properties I'll discuss in this book were first proposed by Apple, Google, and Mozilla, not the W3C or the CSS Working Group. This led to a problem: developers wanted their browsers to support these cool technologies *today,* without having to wait for the long process of W3C recommendation, discussion, and final approval. Everyone knew the bitter lessons of the browser wars of the 90s and the associated clash of conflicting technologies. How could browsers support the very latest technologies proposed by their companies while making it clear that these new properties were experimental, and without conflicting with official declarations from the W3C that might emerge later?

The solution proved workable, but controversial: CSS vendor prefixes.

CSS Vendor Prefixes

To allow CSS3 innovation by browser developers, the web development community agreed that each browser would have its own unique prefix for proposed or experimental CSS properties (see Table 1-1).

Table 1-1. *Unique Browser Prefixes*

Prefix	Browser
-moz-	Firefox
-o-	Opera
-webkit-	Safari/Chrome/Konqueror
-ms-	Internet Explorer 9+

▓ **Note**   The vendor prefixes shown here are not the only ones in existence, just the ones you will need for most purposes. A complete list of vendor prefixes can be found at `http://alrra.github.com/little-helpers/vendor-prefixes/`).

Every browser intended to support an experimental CSS property can do so by placing its own vendor prefix in front of it. Note that these properties are *nonstandard* until they achieve final approval by the W3C. Until that time, they are open to modification and interpretation both by vendors and the W3C itself. Both the property name and the way its value is specified may change rapidly, even in the same browser, as different approaches are considered and standards worked out. For example, up until the release of Safari 5.1/iOS 5.0, the Webkit development team proposed the following as the way to do linear gradients in CSS:

```
body { background-image: -webkit-gradient(
linear,
left bottom,
left top,
color-stop(0.11, rgb(167,9,246)),
color-stop(0.56, rgb(194,242,242)) );
```

Other browsers implemented gradients in different ways. For example, here's how it was done in Firefox:

```
body {
background-image: -moz-linear-gradient(bottom, rgb(167,9,246) 11%,
rgb(194,242,242) 56%);
}
```

These two approaches produced the same result in each browser; under contention was which was the better way to code. In the case of gradients, the W3C took a third way, more closely related to the Firefox method:

```
body {
background-image: linear-gradient(to bottom, rgb(167,9,246) 11%,
rgb(194,242,242) 56%);
}
```

However, because browsers cannot be forced to upgrade retroactively, it is still necessary to include the earlier vendor-prefixed methods to enable support in older versions. In the case of gradients, this includes both methods for Webkit-based browsers, which switched to supporting the now-standard method but kept the vendor prefix for a time.

Convention dictates that the W3C method (the final, expected standard) goes last in the declaration, and that vendor-prefixed versions precede it. The entire declaration for all browsers would be as follows:

```
body {
background-image: -o-linear-gradient(bottom, rgb(167,9,246) 11%,
rgb(194,242,242) 56%);
background-image: -moz-linear-gradient(bottom, rgb(167,9,246) 11%,
rgb(194,242,242) 56%);
background-image: -webkit-linear-gradient(bottom, rgb(167,9,246) 11%,
rgb(194,242,242) 56%);
background-image: -ms-linear-gradient(bottom, rgb(167,9,246) 11%, rgb(194,242,242) 56 %);
background-image: -webkit-gradient(linear, left bottom, left top,
color-stop(0.11, rgb(167,9,246)),
color-stop(0.56, rgb(194,242,242)) );
background-image: linear-gradient(to top, rgb(167,9,246) 11%, rgb(194,242,242)
56%);
}
```

As browsers only pay attention to the CSS they understand, and ignore any CSS they don't, Safari and Chrome will read the -webkit line of the declaration *appropriate to that browser version* and implement it. Later browser versions that understand the final version of the spec will read the last line instead.

It is entirely possible for browsers to support both prefixed and unprefixed CSS properties at the same time. Rules for appearance in a declaration are read from left to right and top to bottom. In the case of a conflict, rules specified *later* take precedence over those written *earlier*. Placing the W3C standard last in the declaration ensures that it will always take precedence if the browser supports it.

While this code may appear somewhat daunting, it is immediately apparent that there is a great deal of repetition within it. With the exception of the deprecated Webkit method, most of the CSS declaration could be easily created by copying and pasting the first line and prepending vendor prefixes to the copies. There are also tools and techniques for automatic generation of vendor-prefixed code, which I will discuss in Chapter 10.

In order to gain support for experimental CSS properties in a particular browser, you *must* include the appropriate vendor prefix and value in your stylesheet. There are just two exceptions:

- The browser allows prefix aliases (discussed in the next section).

- The browser follows the final W3C standard and does not require a prefix.

Thankfully, properties and values for CSS Transforms, Transitions, and Animations have been broadly agreed to since the inception of the modules; as of this writing, every current browser, implements the code the same way, albeit with vendor prefixing.

▨ **Note** On June 6, 2012 the W3C finalized the specification for transitions, animations, and transforms and agreed to let all browser vendors support them without vendor prefixes. Internet Explorer 10 is the first browser to do so, with other browsers expected to follow suit shortly. Older browser versions will still require vendor prefixes.

Vendor Prefixing Issues

While the vendor prefixing system works, it does have several issues. Exceptions and edge cases can be difficult to track and remember. For example, the best current solution to implement hyphenation for paragraphs in all browsers is as follows:

```
p { -ms-word-break: break-all; word-break: break-all; word-break: break-word;
-moz-hyphens: auto; -webkit-hyphens: auto; hyphens: auto; hyphenate: auto;  }
```

As you can see, some of the preceding CSS declaration uses vendor prefixes, but the property names and values do not match the W3C proposal at the end, and different browsers use other properties.

Additionally, some browser vendors have tended to hold on to their proprietary prefixes and have not deprecated them after standards were agreed to, requiring developers to maintain legacy prefixed CSS code.

Finally, lazy developers have tended to implement just one or two vendor prefixes, ignoring other browsers that offer equal support under their own version of the spec. For example, many developers will include -moz and -webbkit prefixed properties in their stylesheets, but forget to add -ms or -o. For this reason, some browsers—most notably, recent versions of Opera—have the capacity to recognize other vendor prefixes. In the case of Opera, this means some -webkit prefixed properties.

▨ **Note** Because a complete CSS declaration that includes every vendor prefix can be very long, code examples in this book will often use just the final expected specification. *In most cases you should not limit prefixed properties to just the examples you see here if you wish to gain complete backward compatibility in all browsers.*

CSS3 Browser Support

CSS3 Transforms are fully supported by the following browser versions, with vendor prefixing:

- Internet Explorer 9 (IE10 does not require prefixes)
- Firefox 3.5 and above
- Chrome 4 and above
- Safari 3.1 and above
- Opera 10.5 and above
- iOS Safari 3.2 and above
- Opera Mobile 11
- Android 2.1 and above

CSS3 Transitions are fully supported by the following browser versions, with vendor prefixing:

- Firefox 4 and above
- Chrome 4 and above
- Safari 3.1 and above
- Opera 10.5 and above
- iOS Safari 3.2 and above
- Opera Mobile 10
- Android 2.1 and above

Internet Explorer 10 supports transitions without prefixing; you can expect very recent versions of other browsers to do the same.

The CSS3 Animation working draft is fully supported by the following browser versions, with vendor prefixing:

- Firefox 5 and above
- Chrome 4 and above
- Safari 4 and above
- Opera 12 and above
- iOS Safari 3.2 and above
- Android 4.0 and above (partial support from 2.1)

Again, Internet Explorer 10 supports CSS Animations without prefixing.

■ **Tip** www.caniuse.com is an excellent resource to keep track of browser support for CSS3.

Limitations of CSS3 Animation

While CSS3 Transforms, Transitions, and Animations are very powerful, there are a few properties that they cannot affect, at least not currently:

- CSS3 cannot control scroll bars or "scroll" the entire body of the document
- Gradients cannot be animated (although this is possible to achieve with SVG or JavaScript).

Design Principles: Progressive Enhancement and Graceful Degradation

One of the design methodologies common to both CSS and JavaScript is *graceful degradation*, also known as *progressive enhancement*. Put simply, the idea is to use CSS to *enhance* a website, not for the site to be utterly dependent on it.

This becomes especially important when you start to animate content. Because CSS3 is only supported in certain browsers, when applying advanced technologies, you should always ask, "If the browser doesn't show what I am trying to achieve, can the site still be used?"

This is problematic for some people, especially clients, who insist that a site should look and perform "exactly the same in every browser." In the age of the iPhone and responsive web design, however, this is no longer a realistic expectation. Instead, you need to treat the addition of advanced CSS to a site as a series of what-if scenarios:

- If you use CSS3 to create an image slideshow on a web page (as shown in Chapter 6), and the browser doesn't support it, what happens? If the user sees a static placeholder image in place of the slideshow, is that alright? Or do you need to use JavaScript as a fallback?

- If you use CSS3 to enhance a site's navigation bar with animation, is it okay that some users won't see the animation? Can they still use the navigation bar without it?

The various examples and tutorials throughout this book will demonstrate different solutions to achieve backward compatibility, as there is no one practice or technique that is applicable in all cases. At the same time, I'll also be emphasizing accessibility; that is, enabling users with different needs and abilities (such as the blind, or site visitors who use a keyboard without a mouse) to access your work.

Why CSS3 Rather Than JavaScript or Flash?

You can find a comprehensive list of advantages and disadvantages of using CSS3 rather than JavaScript or Flash in Table 1-2.

Table 1-2. *CSS3 vs. JavaScript and Flash*

CSS3	
Advantages	**Disadvantages**
Builds on familiar ground; uses an established CSS syntax. Simple to understand.	While historically well-supported in Firefox, Safari, and Chrome, compatibility in IE and Opera is limited to recent builds.
Fastest and smoothest form of animation in a browser, with higher frame rates than JavaScript.	Relatively few graphical tools exist to create animation code, forcing a degree of hand coding. (Although this is changing; see Chapter 10.)
Manipulates existing HTML content, enhancing SEO.	
Flash	
Advantages	**Disadvantages**
Well-established GUI to create animations.	Cannot be played on many mobile devices (most significantly Apple iPhone and iPad together with Android and Windows 8 devices).
Loops, variables, and functions make ActionScript (Flash's scripting language) more powerful than CSS.	Depends on the presence of a plug-in that must be regularly updated by the user.
	Tends to "lock down" content, making it inaccessible to CSS, search engine robots, accessibility devices, such as screen readers, and fair use cases.
JavaScript	
Advantages	**Disadvantages**
Well-supported, with a host of frameworks.	Use of a framework requires an extra HTTP request, slowing page load time.
Works by manipulating HTML elements via the DOM and CSS, familiar to any web developer.	Syntax can be somewhat obtuse, even with a framework.
Loops, variables, and functions make the language more powerful than CSS.	Content generated by JavaScript is not indexed by search engines.

Other Technologies

There exists a degree of confusion about the roles of other new web technologies, particularly in clients, so it is worthwhile discussing what CSS3 Animation is not.

- CSS3 is not HTML5. While the two technologies tend to be spoken of in the same breath, CSS3 is not related to HTML5. Markup is not presentation: CSS3 can be equally applied to XHTML or HTML3.1. In this book, you'll be using HTML5 as your markup, but you don't have to.

- CSS3 is not Canvas. <canvas> is an HTML5 element that creates a JavaScript-accessible "drawing area" on a web page. The location of the <canvas> surface is defined by CSS, but any animation that occurs within it is controlled by JavaScript.

- CSS 3D Transforms are part of the CSS Transforms Module, not Animation. CSS Transforms are used to manipulate the visual perspective of HTML elements. These transformations can be animated, but CSS 3D Transforms (discussed in Chapter 9) are not animations in and of themselves.

- WebGL is not CSS Animation. WebGL is a JavaScript 3D API that manipulates drawings in the `<canvas>` element.

Summary

In this chapter you've learned how CSS is developed and standardized, and the role of the W3C in that process. Beginning web developers sometimes see the W3C as a kind of benign overlord, dictating standards from on high; the reality is that the organization and its various working groups is really an integrator and standardizer of innovations created by browser vendors.

While they remain in an experimental state, new CSS properties are up for grabs when it comes to how they are implemented. To this end, vendor prefixes, specific to each browser, are used to distinguish a browser maker's interpretation of a new CSS property. It is only when the property is standardized by the W3C and support is built into the software that a browser will interpret a nonprefixed version.

While CSS3 Animation, Transitions, and Transforms have a number of significant advantages over the traditional web animation solutions of Flash and JavaScript, their relative newness limits them to fairly recent browser builds, most especially in the case of Internet Explorer and Opera. It is important to consider fallback techniques during development so that users with older browsers or who are reliant on assistive devices such as screen readers do not miss out on your site content. (It is equally important to communicate these issues to clients and other web developers, who may frequently choose from a "word salad" of peripheral or unrelated technologies, such as HTML5, when trying to talk about web animation.)

In the next chapter, I'll introduce the syntax for CSS Transforms and how to create CSS Transitions, the simplest form of CSS3 animation. While there will be a little bit of math, we'll leaven this by comparing CSS3 animations with real-world examples of motion, including classical animation techniques employed by Disney.

■ ■ ■

CHAPTER 2

CSS3 Transforms and Transitions

While CSS Animations can be used to alter almost every aspect of an HTML element (with the exception of the properties listed in the previous chapter), some of the most powerful means of manipulating the presentation of web pages lie in the CSS Transforms and Transitions modules, which are entirely new in CSS3.

CSS Transitions are the very simplest form of animation: a movement between two states. Once you master the fundamental syntax for transitions described in this chapter, you will be able to apply simple, effective animations to images (described in Chapter 3) and user interface elements (described in Chapter 4), and then begin to create more complex keyframed animations (described in Chapter 5 and beyond).

CSS Transforms

There are four main CSS translation functions: translate, rotate, scale, and skew. The functions are combined in the matrix transformation function. You'll apply these transformations to a standard web page layout of an image floated next to a paragraph of text as shown in Listing 2-1.

Listing 2-1. HTML5 Code for a Floated Image

```
<!DOCTYPE html>
<html>
<head>
<title>Simple CSS3 Transformation</title>
</head>
<body>
<p><img src="dudley-storey-statuette.jpg" alt="Student-made statuette of Dudley Storey"
style="width: 300px; height: 300px; float: left; margin: 0 2em 1.4em 0;">Lorem ipsum dolor sit
amet, consectetur adipiscing elit. Suspendisse eu mi tellus. Vestibulum tortor erat, facilisis
in auctor semper, pharetra quis mi...</p>
</body>
</html>
```

The code shown in Listing 2-1 will produce the layout shown in Figure 2-1.

Lorem ipsum dolor sit amet, consectetur adipiscing elit. Nulla eros est, ornare in dignissim vitae, mattis vitae est. In vel justo eget dolor viverra tincidunt. Fusce augue justo, iaculis eu venenatis hendrerit, eleifend consequat augue. Suspendisse neque nisi, lacinia at hendrerit at, imperdiet vel sapien. Donec gravida volutpat suscipit. Duis eu volutpat ante. Mauris vitae diam tortor, nec facilisis sapien. Aliquam malesuada aliquam pharetra.

Duis nisi ligula, lacinia ut porttitor ut, semper et mi. Aenean pulvinar, turpis sit amet blandit mollis, lectus justo elementum lectus, vel lobortis turpis neque id dui. Nunc congue molestie commodo. Fusce imperdiet adipiscing libero, eget ornare nulla dictum id. Curabitur at massa at magna venenatis auctor at imperdiet turpis. Nam dapibus luctus convallis. Proin dapibus ullamcorper odio eget ultricies. Vestibulum quis mauris sit amet magna fermentum malesuada quis quis ligula. Quisque nec est velit, nec lobortis ipsum.

Proin vel pharetra nibh. Vestibulum a nisi odio. Duis in magna vel erat ullamcorper gravida ut id eros. Nam vehicula facilisis adipiscing. Aenean ut libero libero, fermentum pharetra sem. Donec malesuada, sapien vitae feugiat laoreet, ipsum dolor imperdiet ligula, sit amet iaculis lorem nisl quis orci. Donec non justo et dui tristique lobortis. Proin felis lectus, eleifend nec cursus et, ipsum dolor sit amet, consectetur adipiscing elit. Nulla eros est, ornare in dignissim vitae, mattis vitae est. In vel justo eget dolor viverra tincidunt. Fusce augue justo, iaculis eu venenatis hendrerit, eleifend consequat augue. Suspendisse neque nisi, lacinia at hendrerit at, imperdiet vel sapien. Donec gravida volutpat suscipit. Duis eu volutpat ante. Mauris vitae diam tortor, nec facilisis sapien. Aliquam malesuada aliquam pharetra.

Duis nisi ligula, lacinia ut porttitor ut, semper et mi. Aenean pulvinar, turpis sit amet blandit mollis, lectus justo elementum lectus, vel lobortis turpis neque id dui. Nunc congue molestie commodo. Fusce imperdiet adipiscing libero, eget ornare nulla dictum id. Curabitur at massa at magna venenatis auctor at imperdiet turpis. Nam dapibus luctus convallis. Proin dapibus ullamcorper odio eget ultricies. Vestibulum quis mauris sit amet magna fermentum malesuada quis quis ligula. Quisque nec est velit,

Figure 2-1. *An image floated with paragraph text*

With this basic page in place, you can start to apply transforms to the image element.

Rotate

First, you'll transform the image by rotating it (see Listing 2-2). Values for CSS3 rotation transformations can be specified in degrees, gradians, turns or radians, using positive or negative floating-point values to create clockwise or anticlockwise rotation. You must include vendor prefixes to cover all browsers.

Listing 2-2. Inline CSS to Rotate an Image

```
<img src="dudley-storey-statuette.jpg" alt="Statuette of Dudley Storey" style="width: 300px;
height: 300px; float: left; margin: 0 2em 1.4em 0; -moz-transform: rotate(7.5deg); -ms-
transform: rotate(7.5deg); -o-transform: rotate(7.5deg); -webkit-transform: rotate(7.5deg);
transform: rotate(7.5deg); ">
```

The result of the code in Listing 2-2 is shown in Figure 2-2.

Lorem ipsum dolor sit amet, consectetur adipiscing elit. Nulla eros est, ornare in dignissim vitae, mattis vitae est. In vel justo eget dolor viverra tincidunt. Fusce augue justo, iaculis eu venenatis hendrerit, eleifend consequat augue. Suspendisse neque nisi, lacinia at hendrerit at, imperdiet vel sapien. Donec gravida volutpat suscipit. Duis eu volutpat ante. Mauris vitae diam tortor, nec facilisis sapien. Aliquam malesuada aliquam pharetra.

Duis nisi ligula, lacinia ut porttitor ut, semper et mi. Aenean pulvinar, turpis sit amet blandit mollis, lectus justo elementum lectus, vel lobortis turpis neque id dui. Nunc congue molestie commodo. Fusce imperdiet adipiscing libero, eget ornare nulla dictum id. Curabitur at massa at magna venenatis auctor at imperdiet turpis. Proin dapibus luctus convallis. Proin dapibus ullamcorper odio eget ultricies. Vestibulum quis mauris sit amet magna fermentum malesuada quis quis ligula. Quisque nec est velit, nec lobortis ipsum.

Proin vel pharetra nibh. Vestibulum a nisi odio. Duis in magna vel erat ullamcorper gravida ut id eros. Nam vehicula facilisis adipiscing. Aenean ut libero libero, fermentum pharetra sem. Donec malesuada, sapien vitae feugiat laoreet, ipsum dolor imperdiet ligula, sit amet iaculis lorem nisl quis orci. Donec non justo et dui tristique lobortis. Proin felis lectus, eleifend nec cursus et, ipsum dolor sit amet, consectetur adipiscing elit. Nulla eros est, ornare in dignissim vitae, mattis vitae est. Fusce augue justo, iaculis eu venenatis hendrerit, eleifend consequat augue. Suspendisse neque nisi, lacinia at hendrerit at, imperdiet vel sapien. Donec gravida volutpat suscipit. Duis eu volutpat ante. Mauris vitae diam tortor, nec facilisis sapien. Aliquam malesuada aliquam pharetra.

Duis nisi ligula, lacinia ut porttitor ut, semper et mi. Aenean pulvinar, turpis sit amet blandit mollis, lectus justo elementum lectus, vel lobortis turpis neque id dui. Nunc congue molestie commodo. Fusce imperdiet adipiscing libero, eget ornare nulla dictum id. Curabitur at massa at magna venenatis auctor at imperdiet turpis. Nam dapibus luctus convallis. Proin dapibus ullamcorper odio eget ultricies. Vestibulum quis mauris sit amet magna fermentum malesuada quis quis ligula. Quisque nec est velit,

Figure 2-2. *A floated image with a CSS rotate transformation*

While measuring rotation in degrees is the most common approach when writing CSS transformations, CSS3 allows a variety of units, shown in Table 2-1:

Table 2-1. *Possible unit systems for the CSS angle data type*

Unit	CSS	Description	Example
Degrees	deg	360 degrees in a circle	rotate(90deg)
Gradians	grad	Also known as "gons" or "grades". 400 gradians in a circle, making for easier calculations.	rotate(100grad)
Radians	rad	2π radians in a full circle, equal to 6.2831853rad.	rotate(1.57rad)
Turns	turn	A complete rotation = 1 full turn.	rotate(.25turn)

There are a few things to note when floating an image using `rotate`:

- Other HTML content on the page is not affected by transformations: the layout of the paragraphs does not change in response to the image rotation; further rotation of the image would cause it to overlap the text. (Content that reacts to transforms is supported in the CSS Regions Module).

- The Document Object Model (DOM) is similarly unaffected; the value of properties for the transformed element such as `offsetWidth` will also be unchanged.

- CSS transformations essentially impose a state of relative positioning on the affected element; the original space used by the element is retained.

- If the value of the `overflow` property is `scroll` or `auto`, scrollbars will appear as needed to enable you to view content that is transformed outside the visible area.

- The rotation occurs from the computed *center* of the element, the `transform-origin`.

- Other CSS appearance rules applied to the element, such as `box-shadow`, are applied *before* the transformation, so they will be rotated with the effect.

- Rotating the image by 180 degrees will not flip or mirror it; that can be achieved using a hack of the scale transformation, discussed later in this chapter, or a 3D rotation, discussed in Chapter 9.

- You can rotate any HTML content you wish, but from a design perspective it is not recommended that you rotate text: doing so reduces legibility and induces a painful crick in the neck for your readers.

- The unit of measurement needs to be present, even if the amount of rotation is 0. In most CSS measurements, 0 is 0 for any unit, (i.e., width: 0 works as an alternative to width: 0px.) But when rotating to 0, you must specify transform: rotate(0deg); transform: rotate(0) will not work.

As you can see, inline styles for transformations can be lengthy due to the requirement to include vendor prefixes. It is much more common to create transformations separately, as a class or id in an embedded or linked stylesheet (see Listing 2-3).

Listing 2-3. An Embedded CSS Stylesheet for Transforming an Image

```
<!DOCTYPE html>
<html>
<head>
<title>Simple CSS3 Transformation</title>
<style>
img.tilt {
width: 300px; height: 300px; float: left;
-moz-transform: rotate(7.5deg); -o-transform: rotate(7.5deg);
-ms-transform: rotate(7.5deg); -webkit-transform: rotate(7.5deg);
transform: rotate(7.5deg);
}
</style>
</head>
<body>
<p><img src="dudley-storey-statuette.jpg" alt="Statuette of Dudley Storey"
style="margin: 0 2em 1.4em 0; class="tilt">Lorem ipsum dolor sit amet,
consectetur adipiscing elit. Suspendisse eu mi tellus. Vestibulum tortor erat,
facilisis in auctor semper, pharetra quis mi...</p>
</body>
</html>
```

To rotate the image as if it were pinned at its top-right corner, you must move the element's transform-origin to that location, as shown in Listing 2-4.

Listing 2-4. Rotating an Image from a Corner

```
img.tilt {
width: 300px; height: 300px; float: left;
-moz-transform-origin: right top;
-o-transform-origin: right top; -ms-transform-origin: right top;
-webkit-transform-origin: right top; transform-origin: right top;
-moz-transform: rotate(-10deg); -o-transform: rotate(-10deg);
-ms-transform: rotate(-10deg); -webkit-transform: rotate(-10deg);
transform: rotate(-10deg);
}
```

The code in Listing 2-4 will create the result shown in Figure 2-3; note that I've had to change the image's inline style slightly to provide it with more space for the margin on the right-hand side to compensate for the new angle of the image.

Lorem ipsum dolor sit amet, consectetur adipiscing elit. Nulla eros est, ornare in dignissim vitae, mattis vitae est. In vel justo eget dolor viverra tincidunt. Fusce augue justo, iaculis eu venenatis hendrerit, eleifend consequat augue. Suspendisse neque nisi, lacinia at hendrerit at, imperdiet vel sapien. Donec gravida volutpat suscipit. Duis eu volutpat ante. Mauris vitae diam tortor, nec facilisis sapien. Aliquam malesuada aliquam pharetra.

Duis nisi ligula, lacinia ut porttitor ut, semper et mi. Aenean pulvinar, turpis sit amet blandit mollis, lectus justo elementum lectus, vel lobortis turpis neque id dui. Nunc congue molestie commodo. Fusce imperdiet adipiscing libero, eget ornare nulla dictum id. Curabitur at massa at magna venenatis auctor at imperdiet turpis. Nam dapibus luctus convallis. Proin dapibus ullam-corper odio eget ultricies. Vestibulum quis mauris sit amet magna fermentum malesuada quis quis ligula. Quisque nec est velit, nec lobortis ipsum.

Proin vel pharetra nibh. Vestibulum a nisi odio. Duis in magna vel erat ullamcorper gravida ut id eros. Nam vehicula facilisis adipiscing. Aenean ut libero libero, fermentum pharetra sem. Donec malesuada, sapien vitae feugiat laoreet, ipsum dolor imperdiet ligula, sit amet iaculis lorem nisl quis orci. Donec non justo et dui tristique lobortis. Proin felis lectus, eleifend nec cursus et, ipsum dolor sit amet, consectetur adipiscing elit. Nulla eros est, ornare in dignissim vitae, mattis vitae est. In vel justo eget dolor viverra tincidunt. Fusce augue justo, iaculis eu venenatis hendrerit, eleifend consequat augue. Suspendisse neque nisi, lacinia at hendrerit at, imperdiet vel sapien. Donec gravida volutpat suscipit. Duis eu volutpat ante. Mauris vitae diam tortor, nec facilisis sapien. Aliquam malesuada aliquam pharetra.

Figure 2-3. Rotated, floated image with paragraph text

transform-origin takes values the same way background-position and other properties that combine a horizontal and vertical offset do. The values are specified as the horizontal position of the origin point followed by the vertical position, *relative to the element itself.* The values can be specified as keywords (top, center, bottom, left, and right), numerically, or as a combination of the two. They can also be outside the area of the element itself (for example, to create a transformation origin axis above or below the element, as shown in the "card fan" image gallery example in Chapter 3).

The Webkit CSS3 Transform Aliasing Issue

Early versions of Chrome and Safari (up to version 5.1) contain a rendering bug: when transforming some elements, the browsers will not antialias the edges of rotated or skewed HTML content, resulting in so-called "jaggies" or "staircasing" on the edges of images, as shown in Figure 2-4.

Figure 2-4. *Zoomed image, showing aliasing of edges on an image rotated with CSS transform*

There are various techniques for getting around this bug :

- Apply a 1-pixel white border around the element.

- Apply `webkit-backface-visibility: hidden;` to the element.

- Add another transformation to the element, such as `-webkit-transform: rotate(-10deg) translateZ(0);`.

There is no single technique that best addresses the rendering bug in all circumstances, however; the effectiveness of each technique depends on the context of the element being rendered.

Scale

The `scale` transform is something of an oddity when applied to images: given that changing an image's `height` and `width` will have much the same visual result, it might not seem useful. The difference is that `scale` can be applied to *any* HTML element: changing the `width` of a paragraph will reflow the text content, but altering its `scale` will make the text physically larger or smaller.

The value for `scale` is a multiplier: `scale(2)` applied to an element will make it appear twice as wide and twice as high (in other words, four times its normal size), while `scale (.5)` will result in an image that is one-fourth its original size. scale will transform the element equally in all directions. You can also apply scale to ordinal directions: X (horizontal), Y (vertical), and Z (depth).

Flipping Images with scaleX

You can use the scale CSS transformation to effectively mirror HTML elements (usually images, although in principle this technique could be applied to any element). If scale starts at 1, as shown on the left side of the diagram in Figure 2-5, the affected element will grow smaller as you lower the value of scale until you reach 0, when the image disappears. If you push the value into negative territory, the image will begin to grow again, but will appear flipped horizontally, as shown on the right side of Figure 2-5.

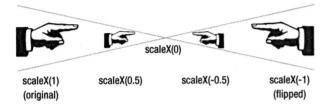

Figure 2-5. *Effect of using small and negative values of scaleX()*

You can use scale to quickly flip an image on a page, rather than processing it through an application such as Adobe PhotoShop to generate a new copy. Listing 2-5 shows how the transformation could be applied to reverse an image of Abraham Lincoln.

Listing 2-5. Flipping an Image with an Inline Transform Style

```
<img src="lincoln.jpg" alt="Abraham Lincoln, 1863" style="width: 389px; height: 480px;
-moz-transform: scaleX(-1); -o-transform: scaleX(-1);  -ms-transform: scaleX(-1);
-webkit-transform: scaleX(-1); transform: scaleX(-1);">
```

Figure 2-6 shows the outcome of the code in Listing 2-5.

Figure 2-6. *Original photograph of Abraham Lincoln (left) flipped using CSS3 scale transform (right)*

Using CSS techniques like this, you can adjust images on the fly instead of having to return to PhotoShop, make the changes, then save and upload the file to the site, and without having to modify any HTML code.

Translate

Like scale, the translate modifier might seem a bit redundant at first: it uses the same coordinate system (and visually, produces the same result) as applying top, left, bottom, and right properties to a relatively positioned element. However, as you will see, translate can make it easier to animate HTML content.

translate(x,y) moves the element in horizontal and vertical directions by using positive or negative values. translateX() moves the element in the horizontal plane, while translateY() moves it vertically.

For example, if you wanted to move the statuette image shown in Figure 2-4 up 4em and to the right by 50px, you'd use the code shown in Listing 2-6.

Listing 2-6. CSS Code for Translating an Image

```
img.tilt {
width: 300px; height: 300px; float: left;
-moz-transform: translate(50px, -4em); -o-transform: translate(50px, -4em);
-ms-transform: translate(50px, -4em); -webkit-transform: translate(50px, -4em);
transform: translate(50px, -4em);
}
```

Skew

Applying skew to an element "shears" it horizontally or vertically and can be useful for imparting an extra sense of speed or motion to an element. Imagine taking the opposite sides of a rectangle (the top and bottom edges, for example, or the left and right sides) and pulling them in different directions, while ensuring that they remain parallel.

The values entered for skew refer to the angle that the *other* sides will be set to. For example, "leaning" an image to the right is a skewX transformation. transform: skewX(21deg) will mean that the left and right edges of the image will be set to 21 degrees from the vertical (see Listing 2-7). Leaning the image to the left still uses skewX, but with a negative value: skewX(-21deg), for example, will set the same edges negative 21 degrees (that is, left) from the vertical. skewY takes the *left* and *right* sides of an element's box and shifts them up and down.

Listing 2-7. CSS Code for Skewing an Image

```
img.tilt {
width: 300px; height: 300px; float: left;
-moz-transform: skewX(21deg); -o-transform: skewX(21deg);
-ms-transform: skewX(21deg); -webkit-transform: skewX(21deg);
transform: skewX(21deg);
}
```

You can see the outcome of Listing 2-7 in Figure 2-7.

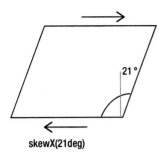

skewX(21deg)

Figure 2-7. A rectangular element skewed with CSS

A combination of both horizontal and vertical skew with appropriate values while translating the element in the corresponding directions can provide the impression that the element forms one side of a box, as shown in Listing 2-8.

Listing 2-8. CSS Code to Transform an Image into One Side of an Isometric Box

```
img.tilt {
width: 300px; height: 300px; float: left;
-moz-transform: skewY(30deg); -o-transform: skewY(30deg);
-ms-transform: skewY(30deg);  -webkit-transform skewY(30deg);
transform: skewY(30deg);
}
```

Combining individual transformations together (for example, a rotation and translation) provides much more power to your CSS and gives you many more possibilities for animation.

Combining Transformations

You can merge transformations for an element in one of two ways: as space-separated values of a transform property, or as values for a matrix property.

To merge transformations as space-separated values of a transform property, use the code shown in Listing 2-9.

Listing 2-9. Multiple Transforms in a Single CSS Declaration

```
img.tilt { width: 300px; height: 300px; float: left;
-moz-transform: translate(50px, -4em) rotate(15deg);
-webkit-transform: translate(50px, -4em) rotate(15deg);
-o-transform: translate(50px, -4em) rotate(15deg);
-ms-transform: translate(50px, -4em) rotate(15deg);
transform: translate(50px, -4em) rotate(15deg); }
```

The process for merging transformations as values for a matrix property is significantly more complicated. Matrix transformations are a little beyond the scope of this book; it's easiest to use a tool to generate the code. The Useragentman Matrix Construction Set (www.useragentman.com/matrix/) and CSS3 Transform Matrix Calculator (www.leeourand.com/test/transform/test/transform.html) offer two ways of doing so. An explanation of matrix transformations can be found at The CSS Matrix Transform for the Mathematically Challenged (www.useragentman.com/blog/2011/01/07/css3-matrix-transform-for-the-mathematically-challenged/)

and at the Opera Web Developer site (http://dev.opera.com/articles/view/understanding-the-css-transforms-matrix). While they have the advantage of being shorter and more efficient, matrix transforms are not human-readable, so I won't use them for the examples in this book.

■ **Note**   Writing separate transforms will *not* work to create a combined transformation.

```
img.tilt { width: 300px; height: 300px; float: left;
transform: translate(50px, -4em);
transform: rotate(15deg);
-webkit-transform: translate(50px, -4em);
-webkit-transform: rotate(15deg); }
```

With the above CSS the browser will follow the *last* applicable line of code; that is, the image will be rotated, but not translated.

CSS Transitions

CSS Transitions are exactly that: a transition from one visual state to another, most often initated by some user event, such as a mouseover on an element. Transitions, in other words, are point-to-point. If you need to animate between more than one state and another you will find that CSS Keyframes are better suited for the job. (CSS Keyframes will be discussed in Chapter 5.)

Note that for the examples in this chapter I'll be using :hover to initiate transitions, but technically *any* modification to the value of an element's property will trigger a transition for that property.

Let's return to the first example and create a simple rotation transition for the image on the page. When the user places their mouse over the image, you want to rotate the element by 7.5 degrees. You'll do this by adding a :hover pseudo class to the .tilt selector (:hover can be applied to every element, not just links), as shown in Listing 2-10.

Listing 2-10. CSS Transform on Hover, no Transition

```
<style>
img.tilt:hover {
-moz-transform: rotate(7.5deg); -o-transform: rotate(7.5deg);
-ms-transform: rotate(7.5deg); -webkit-transform: rotate(7.5deg);
transform: rotate(7.5deg);
}
</style>
```

The code shown in Listing 2-10 will work, but if you try viewing the page in a browser you'll see that there's no animation on mouseover, just an instantaneous flick between one state and the other. You'll create an animation between these states by using the transition property (see Listing 2-11).

Listing 2-11. Smoothing a CSS Transform by Using a Transition

```
img.tilt:hover {
-moz-transform: rotate(7.5deg); -o-transform: rotate(7.5deg);
-ms-transform: rotate(7.5deg); -webkit-transform: rotate(7.5deg);
transform: rotate(7.5deg);
-moz-transition: 2s all; -webkit-transition: 2s all;
-o-transition: 2s all; transition: 2s all;
}
```

The code shown in Listing 2-11 is far more successful: when you mouse over the image you'll see that it now rotates smoothly to its new position. The syntax, repeated with multiple vendor prefixes, is easy to understand, too. The element is rotated over two seconds, and all of its properties can be altered during the transition. Note that the order of the values doesn't matter: you can use 2s all or all 2s.

If you are animating elements over time periods that include fractions of seconds, you can specify the time period as either floating-point values in seconds, or as milliseconds (thousandths of a second), as shown in Listing 2-12.

Listing 2-12. A CSS Transition Measured in Seconds

```
img.tilt:hover {
-moz-transform: rotate(7.5deg); -o-transform: rotate(7.5deg);
-ms-transform: rotate(7.5deg); -webkit-transform: rotate(7.5deg);
transform: rotate(7.5deg);
-moz-transition: 2.35s all; -webkit-transition: 2.35s all;
-o-transition: 2.35s all; transition: 2.35s all;
}
```

This could also be expressed as shown in Listing 2-13.

Listing 2-13. A CSS Transition Measured in Milliseconds

```
img.tilt:hover {
-moz-transform: rotate(7.5deg); -o-transform: rotate(7.5deg);
-ms-transform: rotate(7.5deg); -webkit-transform: rotate(7.5deg);
transform: rotate(7.5deg);
-moz-transition: 2350ms all;
-webkit-transition: 2350ms all; -o-transition: 2350ms all;
transition: 2350ms all;
}
```

While animation timing in milliseconds allows greater precision, the two declarations above achieve the same result—using milliseconds does not create a smoother animation sequence. Very few animations will require accuracy down to one-thousandth of a second, and specifying time in milliseconds usually requires more typing, so I stick with the more familiar seconds format (even for values of less than one second: transition: .35s all, for example). You should use whichever system you feel more comfortable with.

■ **Note**   If you've animated with JavaScript, note the difference here: CSS3 can use floating-point values in seconds *or* milliseconds for timing animations. JavaScript uses milliseconds exclusively, although many JavaScript frameworks used to create animations can use time intervals measured in seconds.

There is just one more improvement to make. You'll notice that after the element has been rotated, moving your mouse off the image returns it instantaneously to its initial state. While that may be the visual effect you seek for web page elements in some circumstances, in most cases it is better to show the element returning to its initial orientation just as smoothly as it arrived in its rotated state.

The solution is slightly counterintuitive: move the `transition` portion of the CSS code from the `:hover` declaration to the *default* state for the image, keeping only the `transform` on the `:hover` declaration (see Listing 2-14).

Listing 2-14. Creating a Smooth Transition to and from a Default State

```
<style>
img.tilt {
width: 300px; height: 300px; float: left;
-moz-transition: 2s all; -webkit-transition: 2s all;
-o-transition: 2s all; transition: 2s all;
}
img.tilt:hover {
-moz-transform: rotate(7.5deg); -o-transform: rotate(7.5deg);
-ms-transform: rotate(7.5deg); -webkit-transform: rotate(7.5deg);
transform: rotate(7.5deg);
}
</style>
```

The idea is simple: placing the `transition` property on the class declaration implies that any transition is in effect both *from* and *back to* this state. The previous example placed the transition on the `:hover` declaration, meaning that it was only effective on mouse hover, not during the return to the normal state.

You'll also notice that the transition can be interrupted if you move your mouse to and from the area of the image; its motion will be reversed smoothly. You can shortcut the code further by only specifying the time for the transition (see Listing 2-15).

Listing 2-15. Timed Rotation in a CSS Transformation

```
img.tilt {
width: 300px; height: 300px; float: left;
-moz-transition: 2s;
-webkit-transition: 2s; -o-transition: 2s;
transition: 2s; }
img.tilt:hover {
-moz-transform: rotate(7.5deg); -o-transform: rotate(7.5deg);
-ms-transform: rotate(7.5deg); -webkit-transform: rotate(7.5deg);
transform: rotate(7.5deg);
}
```

As you've seen, creating a smooth and simple animation is easy with CSS3 Transitions. You can modify and animate almost every aspect of an element's appearance that CSS properties provide access to. The transitions I've shown you so far have changed only one aspect of an element at a time, and always in the same fashion. To create richer animations you can combine multiple property transitions for the same element that occur at different times and speeds.

Delaying and Combining Transition Effects

A transition event can be delayed by adding a `transition-delay`, either as a separate property or appended to the values for `transform`:

```
-moz-transition: 2s 4s;
-webkit-transition: 2s 4s; -o-transition: 2s 4s; transition: 2s 4s;
```

Note that the delay takes effect at both the start of the animation and the start of the element's reversal to its beginning point. The animation will not begin until four seconds after the cursor has been held over the image; once it is fully rotated, the element will stay in place for four seconds before returning to its default orientation. (Also note that the animation will not begin until the mouse has been held over the image for *at least* four seconds).

You can animate several CSS properties at the same time by adding them to the `:hover` state (see Listing 2-16).

Listing 2-16. Several CSS Properties Transitioned Simultaneosly

```
<style>
img.tilt {
width: 300px; height: 300px; float: left;
-moz-transition: 2s;
-ms-transition: 2s;
-o-transition: 2s;
-webkit-transition: 2s;
transition: 2s;
}
img.tilt:hover {
-moz-transform: rotate(15deg);
-o-transform: rotate(15deg); -ms-transform: rotate(15deg);
-webkit-transform: rotate(15deg); transform: rotate(15deg);
opacity: .3;
}
</style>
```

The properties can be given separate timings in the animation by stating `transition-duration` as a separate property with comma-separated values. Let's say you wanted to move the image to the right on hover, and fade it out at the same time, but with the fade taking half the time that the movement does (see Listing 2-17).

Listing 2-17. A CSS3 Transition of Multiple Properties with Different Timings for Each

```
<style>
img.tilt {
width: 300px; height: 300px; float: left; position: relative;
-moz-transition-property: opacity, left;
-o-transition-property: opacity, left;
-webkit-transition-property: opacity, left;
transition-property: opacity, left;
-moz-transition-duration: 2s, 4s;
-o-transition-duration: 2s, 4s;
-webkit-transition-duration: 2s, 4s;
transition-duration: 2s, 4s;
}
```

```
img.tilt:hover {
opacity: .2; left: 60px;
}
</style>
```

I've added `position: relative` in order to be able to move the element by changing the value of its `left`, and improved the efficiency of the animation by clearly stating the properties to be animated. (Obviously you don't have to prefix properties that are well-supported across all browsers, such as `opacity`.) You'll notice that the left-to-right animation may not be particularly smooth in some browsers. Let's change the animated property to `translate`, as shown in Listing 2-18.

Listing 2-18. A CSS3 Translation Transition

```
<style>
img.tilt {
width: 300px; height: 300px; float: left;
-moz-transition-property: opacity, translateX;-o-transition-property: opacity, translateX;
-webkit-transition-property: opacity, translateX;
transition-property: opacity, translateX;
-moz-transition-duration: 2s, 4s;
-o-transition-duration: 2s, 4s;
-webkit-transition-duration: 2s, 4s;
transition-duration: 2s, 4s;
}
img.tilt:hover {
opacity: .2;
-webkit-transform: translateX(60px);
-moz-transform: translateX(60px); -ms-transform: translateX(60px);
-o-transform: translateX(60px); transform: translateX(60px);
}
</style>
```

You may find that the movement is now smoother; `translate` is a good alternative for animating the movement of HTML elements via manipulation of `absolute` or `relative` positioning.

Introducing Easing Functions

Observe closely the movement of the image on mouseover in the animations you have created so far: there's something a little special about it (lengthening the time value for the animation may help make this clearer). The motion of the image is not mechanical, but organic: from its default position, the picture speeds up as it rotates, reaches a constant speed for a moment, then slows down before it comes to rest.

In animation, this kind of motion is referred to as *ease in/ease out*. It is the motion of objects in the everyday world. For example, no car, no matter how powerful, can attain a 0–60 speed record of 0 seconds. Every moving object accelerates to a certain velocity; at the end of its travel (outside of an extreme situation, such as a car crashing into a brick wall at top speed) the object will slow down before coming to a stop.

In CSS3 animation, *ease* transitions are the default; there's no need to state that you are using them. If you want to use animation with a more "mechanical" feel to it, you can start by specifying a `linear` transition (see Listing 2-19).

Listing 2-19. CSS for a Linear Rotation Transition

```
<style>
img.tilt {
width: 300px; height: 300px; float: left;
-moz-transform: rotate(7.5deg); -o-transform: rotate(7.5deg);
-ms-transform: rotate(7.5deg); -webkit-transform: rotate(7.5deg);
transform: rotate(7.5deg);
-moz-transition: 2s transform linear;
webkit-transition: 2s transform linear; -o-transition: 2s transform linear;
transition: 2s transform linear;
}
</style>
```

You'll see that the motion of the image on mouseover is now far more mechanical.

Transition Timing Functions and Bezier Curves

linear and ease are just two forms of what are referred to as *timing functions*, that is, descriptions of the way in which an object gets from A to B in a straight line. These timing functions may be graphed in a mathematical expression known as Bezier curves.

For example, if you graphed the motion of an element during its transition from 0 to 15 degrees under linear conditions, with time assigned to the horizontal axis and the angle of the image assigned to the vertical, the graph for linear animation would look like Figure 2-8. As time progresses, the angle of rotation increases in lockstep with the passing seconds, creating a constant rate of motion.

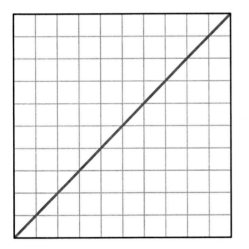

Figure 2-8. *Graph for linear animation: time on x (horizontal) axis, distance/angle on y (vertical) axis. Note the direct relationship*

Removing the linear keyword from the declaration returns the animation to its natural easing state, which when plotted on the same axes would look more like Figure 2-9.

23

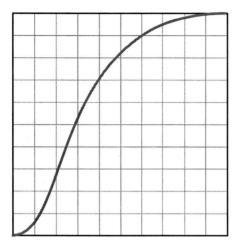

Figure 2-9. *Easing timing function: time on x axis, distance on y axis*

As you can see, the angle of rotation changes slowly in the first moments of the eased animation; toward the middle of the transition, the rate of change increases markedly, reaches a "terminal velocity", then slows down until the sequence reaches its conclusion.

There are several keywords that can be used as a shortcut for common transition motions (see Table 2-2).

Table 2-2. *Keyword Alternatives to Common Cubic-Bezier Timing Functions*

Keyword	Graph	Cubic-Bezier	Description
linear		0, 0, 1, 1	Instant start and stop; constant velocity through the range of motion.
ease		0.25, 0.1, 0.25, 1	Swift start, accelerating quickly; slow transition to stop at end.

(continued)

Table 2-2. (*continued*)

Keyword	Graph	Cubic-Bezier	Description
ease-in		0.42, 0, 1, 1	Slow start, acceleration climbing to a sudden stop.
ease-out		0, 0, 0.58, 1	Instant start to animation, motion slows down towards end.
ease-in-out		0.42, 0, 0.58, 1	Element is eased in and out during animation: a slow, smooth start briefly attaining a constant velocity during the middle of the transition before slowing to a stop.

As you can see, all easing curves have a mathematical equivalent in the form of a cubic-bezier expression: a number pair in which each set of floating-point digits describes a point in coordinate space, forming a line that creates a transition curve. (Note that the points at the termination of the curve on either end cannot be moved or defined).

For an ease-in-out curve, the points look like Figure 2-10.

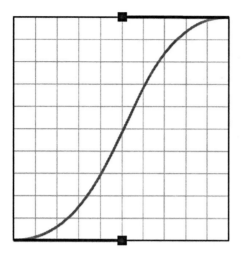

Figure 2-10. *Bezier curve for an ease-in-out animation effect*

Expressed in CSS, Figure 2-10 looks like this:

```
transition-timing-function: cubic-bezier(0.42, 0, 0.58, 1);
```

Understanding the cubic-bezier function allows you to create an almost infinite variety of custom easing curves for your CSS animations. It is even possible to give the points negative values or values greater than 1 to create extreme easing curves, which you can see in Figure 2-11.

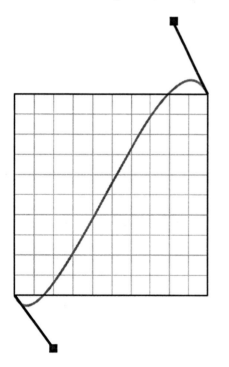

Figure 2-11. *Bezier curve with negative and greater-than-1 values, creating a "push-pull" animation effect*

In CSS, Figure 2-11 looks like this:

```
transition: all 2000ms cubic-bezier(0.280, -0.315, 0.685, 1.390);
```

The use of such values creates animations with a "spring" or "bounce" to them, also known as *push-pull* animations. I will explore the uses of such animations in Chapter 4.

■ **Tip**   Ceaser (`http://matthewlein.com/ceaser/`), and Cubic (`http://cssglue.com/cubic`) are excellent tools for generating CSS easing code from graphically manipulated cubic-bezier curves. Both include a testing service to allow you to see the visual result of changes. Peter Beverloo's resource (`http://peter.sh/experiments/css3-transition-timing-functions/`) is also useful, especially in visualizing the step function.

Animating in Steps

It's also possible to animate an element in steps, rather than as a smooth transition. (Think of the sudden, incremental motion of the second hand on a clock). These are created through the steps function and variants. Here I'll economize the code by showing just the CSS3 code for standard properties, Firefox and Webkit.

Let's say that you have an h1 you want to animate on mouseover (see Listing 2-20).

Listing 2-20.   Transition Sequence in Steps for a Heading

```
<style>
h1 {
        font-family: Futura; "Arial Black", Arial, sans-serif;
        text-align: center;
        }
h1:hover {
        -moz-transition: 4s all steps(3, end);
        -webkit-transition: 4s all steps(3, end);
        transition: 4s all steps(3, end);
        -moz-transform: translateX(400px);
        -webkit-transform: translateX(400px);
        transform: translateX(400px);
        }
</style>
```

The code in Listing 2-20 will animate all h1 elements in a series of three "jumps" over four seconds after a two-second delay, with no visible motion between each step. Other variations are possible, as shown in Table 2-3.

Table 2-3. *Step Values for CSS3 Transitions*

Function	Graph	Description
steps(3)		Animation over x number of steps, (steps(3) is illustrated in the graph). Pauses at start. Equivalent to steps(x, end).
steps(3), end		Element is still at start, paused at the end.
steps(x), start		Instant start to animation, element is paused at the end.

Adding Support for Mobile Devices in CSS3 Transitions

So far you've only activated transforms on :hover. That is by far the most common pseudo-class with which to start a transition, but it is not the only one, as you'll see in Chapter 3.

:hover can pose two issues for browsers installed on mobile devices:

- The user's fingertip may obscure animations, particularly on smaller screens.

- Some devices do not support :hover (which makes sense as, strictly speaking, all current mobile platforms rely on direct touch). Instead, they cover simple user interaction with :focus.

If you choose to use :hover, you should cover the possibility of :focus-only mobile platforms by using a grouped selector, as shown in the following code:

```
img.tilt:hover, img.tilt:focus {
-moz-transform: rotate(7.5deg); -o-transform: rotate(7.5deg);
-ms-transform: rotate(7.5deg); -webkit-transform: rotate(7.5deg);
transform: rotate(7.5deg);
}
```

Summary

In this chapter you've learned the syntax for CSS3 transforms: scale, rotate, skew, and translate, including how to flip images and combine transformations. I also covered the code for the simplest form of animation, CSS3 Transitions, showing you how to create transitions, how to modify their timing and delays, and two common ways to initiate them.

The movement and timing of transitions is most commonly controlled through Bezier curves, although it is also possible to use the steps function and keyword shortcuts.

In the next chapter, we'll be exploring how to apply these animation techniques to image elements.

CHAPTER 3

CSS3 Transitions for Images

The most common uses for CSS3 transitions on web pages are, first, generating visual effects for user interface (UI) elements (discussed in the next chapter) and, second, creating brief animated effects for images. In this chapter, you'll use the syntax of the Transitions module to enhance images and their captions by animating them. These techniques demonstrate easy methods for visually enhancing your web pages, making image content and associated information more interactive while minimizing screen "real estate": an important consideration in the age of mobile web development.

Simple Image CrossFade Effect

The first transition you will work on will demonstrate many of the fundamental concepts used in subsequent exercises: positioning images that are exactly the same size on top of each other and initiating events on :hover (see Figure 3-1).

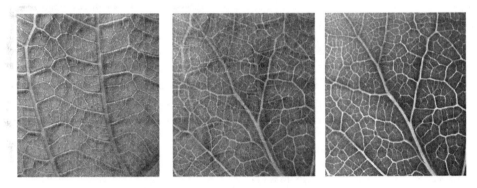

Figure 3-1. A cross-fade effect using a transitioned opacity

There are a few possible ways to achieve the effect shown in Figure 3-1:

- *Option 1*: Specify the first image as the CSS background of a container element, with the second image inside the element itself.

- *Option 2*: Create a container element with position: relative that holds both images, with the second image having position: absolute.

- *Option 3*: Specify both images as backgrounds and transition between them.

All three approaches have their advantages and disadvantages. The first and third methods are potentially quicker to create and more responsive, but are less accessible. Using the first method also means that any changes to the images will have to be made in different places, as one image will exist solely in CSS and the other as an HTML element. The second option may involve a little more code, but has the benefit of keeping both pictures as <img> elements and thus remains more accessible. The third option is technically outside the spec as of this writing, but has perhaps the greatest ease of use.

I will demonstrate all three methods using photographs supplied by Ton Rulkens (www.flickr.com/photos/47108884@N07/4595559479/) and Peter Shanks (www.flickr.com/photos/botheredbybees/1954163161/), used with permission.

Both of the images must be exactly the same size. There are several ways of achieving this:

- Crop the images to the same dimension in an application such as Adobe PhotoShop (this is the most obvious solution).

- You can modify the width and height of the images through CSS or HTML attributes, although this often leads to visual distortion.

- You can set a width and height on the div and use overflow:hidden to trim off portions of the images that fall outside this area.

- If both images are represented as elements in the code, you can use the same CSS clip values for each.

Option 1: First Image As a CSS Background

The HTML for this option is very simple, as shown in Listing 3-1.

Listing 3-1. HTML Option 1 to Create Two Layered Images

```
<div class=crossfade>
        <img src=jatropha-hybrid.jpg alt="Jatropha hybrid leaf">
</div>
```

■ **Note**   HTML5 code samples shown in this book are in "minified" syntax to save space. Elements are closed only when needed and attribute values are only quoted if they contain spaces.

The CSS shown in Listing 3-2 is also very simple.

Listing 3-2. CSS to Create a Cross-fade Effect for HTML Option 1

```
div.crossfade { background: url(leaf-veins.jpg); background-size: cover; }
div.crossfade, div.crossfade img  { width: 418px; height: 500px;  }
div.crossfade img { transition: 3s opacity ease-out; }
div.crossfade img:hover { opacity: 0; }
```

Option 2: Both Images As HTML Elements

Alternatively, you can stack both images inside a single container as individual pictures; the HTML is shown in Listing 3-3.

Listing 3-3. HTML Option 2 to Create Layered Images

```
<div class=crossfade>
        <img src=leaf-veins.jpg alt="Red-veined leaf">
        <img src=jatropha.jpg alt="Jatropha hybrid leaf">
</div>
```

Rather than potentially complicating your HTML by attaching a class to the second image, you will use an nth-child pseudo-selector to alter it, as shown in Listing 3-4.

Listing 3-4. CSS to Create a Cross-fade Effect for HTML Option 2

```
div.crossfade { position: relative; }
div.crossfade, div.crossfade img { width: 418px; height: 500px; }
div.crossfade img:nth-child(2) { position:absolute; left:0; top:0; transition:
3s opacity ease-out; }
div.crossfade img:nth-child(2):hover { opacity: 0; }
```

Option 3: Both Images As Backgrounds

While the easiest to code, this option is also the most daring: it is outside the current specification (and, as of this writing, only supported in Chrome). In this case, the containing div is utterly devoid of content, and everything is achieved via CSS, as shown in Listing 3-5.

Listing 3-5. CSS to Create an Image Cross-fade Effect (Option 3)

```
div.crossfade { width: 418px; height: 500px; transition: 3s background-image ease-out;
background-image: url(leaf-veins.jpg); }
div.crossfade:hover { background-image: url(jatropha.jpg);  }
```

If you were willing to push your code even further, an alternative approach would be to use the same empty div with the CSS4 cross-fade property, shown in Listing 3-6.

Listing 3-6. CSS4 Cross-fade Used to Create an Image Transition

```
div.crossfade { width: 418px; height: 500px;
background-image: -webkit-cross-fade(url(jatropha.jpg), url(leaf-veins.jpg),0);
transition: 2s background-image linear; }
div.crossfade:hover { background-image: -webkit-cross-fade(url(jatropha.jpg),
url(leaf-veins.jpg),100); }
```

As its name implies, cross-fade is a more efficient approach, but with limited practical application at this time; rather than faking a dissolve effect by transitioning opacity, cross-fade processes the images with the appropriate algorithm.

CSS4? WHAT YOU TALKIN' ABOUT, WILLIS?

As CSS3 is becoming mainstream in browsers, the W3C's attention has moved to the next phase of CSS development, which includes new selectors and appearance rules for images and gradients. Browser support (as of this writing) is limited and experimental, but growing.

Most relevant to this section is the CSS4 Image Values and Replaced Content Module, of which you can read an overview at http://dev.w3.org/csswg/css4-images/. There's also a module for backgrounds and borders (http://dev.w3.org/csswg/css4-background/) as well as text (http://dev.w3.org/csswg/css4-text/).

It is almost inevitable that in the near future the term "CSS4" will become as broadly misunderstood and misused as "CSS3" is today, as I discussed in Chapter 1.

A Simple Image Gallery Enhanced with CSS3

For your second example, you'll create an image thumbnail gallery with HTML and enhance the display of large images in the gallery with CSS3 transitions (see Figure 3-2).

Falls in Dundas Peak, Ontario, Canada, taken by Paul Bica

Figure 3-2. *A simple image gallery*

You'll need at least three pairs of images. Each pair will consist of a thumbnail image and a full-size version of the same image. The large version can be whatever size you wish, so long as it is reasonable; I'd suggest making the thumbnails roughly 150 x 150 pixels in size. To keep your file organization clear, follow a naming convention. For example, if the full-size image is x.jpg, name the paired thumbnail x_thumb.jpg, both stored in an images folder.

The HTML Markup

Your goal is to keep the HTML used in the gallery as clean and simple as possible. To that end, you'll use a definition list as the basis for your markup. The definition list is made to contain pairs of elements: one (the definition term) for your thumbnail, the other (the definition declaration) for the large image that it matches.

Assembling your content in the markup relative to your folders, the HTML for the page would look something like Listing 3-7 (using images featured in the previous exercise, with an additional photograph by Paul Bica (www.flickr.com/photos/dexxus/4137841698/).

Listing 3-7. HTML5 for a Simple Image Gallery

```
<!DOCTYPE html>
<html lang=en>
<head>
<meta charset=utf-8>
<title>CSS3 Gallery</title>
<style>
        body { background: #234; }
</style>
</head>
<body>
<dl id=gallery>
        <dt><img src=jatropha_thumb.jpg alt="Jatropha Leaf Thumbnail">
        <dd><img src=jatropha.jpg alt="Jatropha Leaf Large">
        <dt><img src=leaf-veins_thumb.jpg alt="Leaf Veins Thumbnail">
        <dd><img src=leaf-veins.jpg alt="Leaf Veins">
        <dt><img src=cascada_thumb.jpg alt="Cascada Thumbnail">
        <dd><img src=cascada.jpg alt="Cascada Large">
</dl>
</body>
</html>
```

The Initial CSS

The CSS used here should be fairly self-explanatory: you're positioning the definition list `relative` so that the large, absolutely-positioned images are organized in relation to the list, not the body of the document. Positioning the large images absolutely also means that you can stack them in the exact same point, and that the rest of the document—including the thumbnails—will act as though the full-size images are not there at all. Finally, you hide the large images with `visibility: hidden.`, and reveal them again by using a `:hover` selector on the dt elements with an adjacent combinator, as shown in Listing 3-8.

Listing 3-8. CSS for a Simple Image Gallery

```
dl#gallery { position: relative; }
dl#gallery dt img { width: 150px; height: 150px; margin: 2.2em; }
dl#gallery dd { position: absolute; left: 200px; top: 2.2em; visibility: hidden; }
dl#gallery dt:hover + dd { visibility: visible; }
```

Moving your mouse over the thumbnail image causes the large image it is paired with in the definition list to appear immediately. However, there is a UI issue that you need to address before you can bring animation to the gallery.

Improving the Gallery

What you've made so far works, but it's a little clunky: you'll notice that placing your mouse to the right of the thumbnail image makes the associated large image appear immediately. You'll fix both of these issues with a few more lines of CSS, changing from hiding the large images with `visibility` (which can't be animated) to `opacity` (which can) while sharing the size of the definition terms with the thumbnail images, as shown in Listing 3-9.

Listing 3-9. CSS for an Image Gallery Enhanced with Transitions

```
dl#gallery dd { position: absolute; left: 200px; top: 2.2em; opacity: 0;
transition: .85s opacity linear; }
dl#gallery dt:hover + dd { opacity: 1; }
```

Now the large images will fade in smoothly as you move the mouse over the thumbnail images.

Adding Captions

It's very helpful to users if they can read image captions. That doesn't require adding any extra tags in this case, just the caption content and CSS. I'll modify one of the <dt><dd> pairs as an example, shown in Listing 3-10.

Listing 3-10. HTML Example for a Simple Captioned Image

```
<dt><img src=jatropha_thumb.jpg alt="Jatropha Leaf Thumbnail">
<dd><img src=jatropha.jpg alt="Jatropha Leaf Large">A closeup photograph of a Jatropha Hybrid
```

Your CSS must also change in response (see Listing 3-11).

Listing 3-11. CSS for a Simple Captioned Image

```
dl#gallery dd { position: absolute; left: 200px; top: 2.2em; opacity: 0;
text-align: center; font-family: Futura, Arial, sans-serif; color: white;
transition: .85s opacity linear; }
dl#gallery dd img { display: block; margin: auto; padding-bottom: 1.2em; }
```

In this case your captions will fade in with the images. It's also common to animate the captions separately from the images, which you'll do in the next exercise.

Changing the Initiating Event

While :hover works to initiate the fade-in of the large image in the gallery, it may seem more natural for users to *click* the thumbnail. There, you have something of a problem: there is no direct equivalent to the JavaScript onclick event handler in CSS. However, there are a few alternatives in this case.

:active

While it is most strongly associated with links, it is possible to use the :active pseudo-class to initiate the transition, as shown in Listing 3-12.

Listing 3-12. CSS for an Effect on Mouse-down

```
dl#gallery dt:active + dd { opacity: 1; }
```

You'll see the primary disadvantage of this approach immediately: the large image only appears as long as the mouse button is held down over the thumbnail.

:target

The use of :target may be the most effective pseudo-selector in this instance, although it does require some addition to your markup. :target derives from the use of traditional "anchors" of id values, detecting clicks on elements linked to those ids.

Your HTML changes to that shown in Listing 3-13.

Listing 3-13. HTML for an Image Gallery with :target

```
<dl id=gallery>
<dt><a href=#jatropha><img src=jatropha_thumb.jpg alt="Jatropha Leaf Thumbnail"></a>
<dd id=jatropha><img src=jatropha.jpg alt="Jatropha Leaf Large">
A closeup photograph of a Jatropha Hybrid leaf
<dt><a href=#veins><img src=leaf-veins_thumb.jpg alt="Leaf Veins Thumbnail"></a>
<dd id=veins><img src=leaf-veins.jpg alt="Leaf Veins">
Closeup photgraph of leaf veins
<dt><a href=#cascada><img src=cascada_thumb.jpg alt="Cascada Thumbnail"></a>
<dd id=cascada><img src=cascada.jpg alt="Cascada Large">
Falls in Dundas Peak, Ontario, Canada
</dl>
```

Under normal circumstances a link to an anchor would force the page to scroll to the location of the id with a visual jump; that is avoided in this case because the dd elements are absolutely positioned near the top of the page.

Only one line of the CSS requires modification. Your :hover declaration changes as shown in Listing 3-14.

Listing 3-14. CSS for an Image Gallery with :target

```
dd#jatropha:target, dd#veins:target, dd#cascada:target { opacity: 1; }
```

This approach also has the advantage of modifying the URL, meaning that users may be led to particular images through the use of links with appended ids. For example, www.yourdomain.com/gallery.html#cascada would bring up the last image in the gallery automatically.

Simple Popup Image Captions

It is also possible to display the caption of an image on mouseover, either in a gallery or as part of a user interface. The ideal markup for this is either a definition list, as in the previous example, or a <figure> and <figcaption>, which are the elements you'll use for this next example, as shown in Figure 3-3 and Listing 3-15. (I'm using photographs by Bradley Davis (www.flickr.com/photos/backpackphotography/244716694/) and Wolfgang Staudt (www.flickr.com/photos/wolfgangstaudt/). If you decide to use your own images, make sure they are of a similar size.)

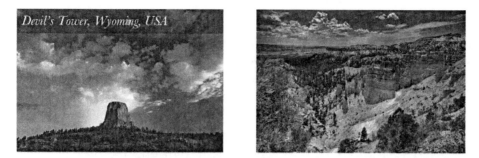

Figure 3-3. Animated image captions

In this case, the captions are descriptions of the image, but this technique could also be used for the graphical navigation for a site (see Chapter 4).

Listing 3-15. HTML5 Figure and Figcaption Code

```
<figure>
        <img src=devils-tower.jpg alt="A photo of Devil's Tower, inWyoming, USA">
        <figcaption>Devil's Tower, Wyoming, USA</figcaption>
</figure>
<figure style=left:550px>
        <img src=sunrise-point.jpg alt="A photo of Sunrise Point, Bryce National
Park, Utah, USA">
        <figcaption>Bryce National Park, Utah, USA</figcaption>
</figure>
```

You're going to do a few things in the CSS. First, the images and the figure element surrounding them should be set to the same size and floated side-by-side. You'll also style the captions before hiding them with more CSS.

REM: NOT THE BAND

Traditionally, fonts on web pages have been sized in pixels, percentages, or ems. The latter two have generally been the preferred approach because they are inherently scalable. Since 1em is literally the width of the M character, making paragraph text 20% larger was as easy as stating that the font-size for the p selector was 1.2em. Using em also makes it easy to proportionally size the space between elements as font sizes increase and decrease. For example, you set the gutter between an image and the text surrounding it by measuring the image's margin in em units, creating a visual relationship between body copy and illustrations.

The one issue with using em as a measurement system in web pages is that it compounds, due to the fact that the unit is always set *relative to the font size of the parent element*. Setting li elements to 1.2em in size is fine until you nest a list inside it: the content of the inner li will be rendered at 1.4em in size.

rem (for *root em*) gets around this problem by measuring itself relative to the root element—that is, the html element. This means that you can declare a single font size on the html selector and scale everything relative to that, as shown in Listing 3-16.

Listing 3-16. rem Font Sizing for a Document

```
html { font-size: 62.5% }
body { font-size: 1.4rem; }
h1 { font-size: 2.4rem; }
```

This also translates nicely to pixels: in the stylesheet above, body text on the page will be equivalent to 14px in size and h1 elements rendered at 24 pixels.

Browser support for rem is surprisingly good: all recent browsers that support CSS Transforms (Safari 5+, Chrome, Firefox 3.6+, IE9+, and Opera 11.6+) also support the rem unit).

Now let's look at basic CSS for a figure and caption (see Listing 3-17).

Listing 3-17. Basic CSS for a Figure and Caption

```
figure { float: left; }
figure, figure img { width: 500px; height: 333px; }

figcaption {
font-family: Baskerville, "Baskerville Old Face", Garamond, "Times New Roman", serif;
font-style: italic; background: rgba(0,0,0,0.4);
font-size: 2rem; padding: 0.8rem; color: #fff;
}
```

At this stage, the page will look something like Figure 3-4.

Figure 3-4. *Images with positioned captions, prior to being hidden*

Now that they are styled, you'll hide the captions by using overflow: hidden on the figure element. At the same time, you need to position the caption. For the images in this example, bringing the captions down from the top will probably look the best. There are a few possible methods for locating the captions. I will use relative positioning and a value for bottom that is slightly greater than the height of the image plus the height of the caption (see Listing 3-18).

▪ **Tip** It's a good idea to check that the relocation of an element works before adding in transitions.

Listing 3-18. CSS to Hide and Position a Caption

```
figure { float: left; }
figure, figure img { width: 500px; height: 333px; overflow: hidden; }
figcaption {
font-family: Baskerville, Garamond, "Times New Roman", serif;
font-style: italic; background: rgba(0,0,0,0.4); font-size: 2rem;
padding: 0.8rem; color: #fff;  position: relative;  bottom: 400px;
}
figure:hover figcaption { bottom: 340px; }
```

Finally, you'll add in the transition of the caption, as shown in Listing 3-19.

Listing 3-19. CSS to Transition a Caption

```
figcaption {
font-family: Baskerville, Garamond, "Times New Roman", serif;
font-style: italic; background: rgba(0,0,0,0.4);
font-size: 2rem; padding: 0.8rem; color: #fff;
position: relative;  bottom: 400px;
transition: 2s all; }
```

■ **Note**   I've kept our images accessible by using descriptive filenames and alt attribute values. This is very important: always remember that not everyone will be able to see or interact with your designs.

Image Card Stack and Fan Reveal

As web pages become more complex, they become more difficult to summarize and illustrate. If you've created an extensive gallery page, it can be very difficult to choose just one image to spark visitors' interest. One possible solution is to use several images, displayed either in a keyframed *slider* gallery (as shown in Chapter 5) or an interactive display. In this case, I'll visibly stack several photographs on top of each other, revealing them on mouseover to create greater interest and understanding of the linked content (see Figure 3-5).

Figure 3-5. *An animated card fan effect*

Again, you will use images of the same size to produce the best results, as shown in Listing 3-20.

Listing 3-20. HTML for an Animated Image Card Fan Effect

```
<div id=cardfan>
        <img src=bike.jpg alt="A photograph of a bicycle parked on Italian street">
        <img src=florence.jpg alt="A photograph of bridge in Florence, Italy">
        <img src=roma.jpg alt="A photograph of a ruined aqueduct outside Rome">
</div>
```

You've wrapped the images in a container element to make them easier to reference and control via CSS. The div and the images it contains are the same size. You'll also center-align the container to the page while styling and stacking the images inside (see Listing 3-21).

Listing 3-21. Basic CSS for a Card Fan Effect

```
#cardfan, #cardfan img { width: 640px; height: 480px; }
#cardfan { margin: 0 auto; }
#cardfan img { border: 32px solid #ffe;
box-shadow: 12px 12px 10px rgba(0, 0, 0, 0.2);
position: absolute; }
```

You want to have the images fan out when the user hovers over them; you can achieve this by rotating the *first* and *last* images in the stack by 12 degrees through the use of the :first-child and :last-child pseudo-classes, as shown in Listing 3-22.

Listing 3-22. Rotation of the First and Last Images in a Card Stack Effect

```
#cardfan:hover img:first-child {
    transform: rotate(12deg);
}
#cardfan:hover img:last-child {
    transform: rotate(-12deg);
}
```

The code in Listing 3-22 will produce the image shown in Figure 3-6.

Figure 3-6. Stacked images rotated with CSS transforms around their respective centers

As you can see, the image rotates around its center. In this case, you want the images to be slightly fanned, so you'll need to move the axis of transformation *below* the images (see Listing 3-23).

Listing 3-23. Offsetting the Transform Origin for Images

```
#cardfan img { border: 32px solid #ffe;
    box-shadow: 12px 12px 10px rgba(0, 0, 0, 0.2);
    position: absolute;
    transform-origin: center 600px;
}
```

The code in Listing 3-23 will produce the output shown in Figure 3-7.

Figure 3-7. Stacked images rotated around an offset origin, highlighted with crosshairs

Now you can truly fan the cards out, applying a transition at the same time, as shown in Listing 3-24. (Note that I've altered some values to increase the fan effect.)

Listing 3-24. Full CSS for an Animated Card Fan Gallery

```
#cardfan, #cardfan img { width: 640px; height: 480px;
transition: .6s transform ease-out;
}
#cardfan { margin: 0 auto; }
#cardfan img { border: 32px solid #ffe;
box-shadow: 12px 12px 10px rgba(0, 0, 0, 0.2);
position: absolute;
transform-origin: center 1200px;
}
div#cardfan:hover img:first-child {
    transform: rotate(24deg);
}
div#cardfan:hover img:last-child {
    transform: rotate(-24deg);
}
```

You could also link the images to a gallery page, as shown in Listing 3-25.

Listing 3-25. A Linked Card Fan Gallery

```
<div id=cardfan>
        <a href=gallery.html>
                <img src=bike.jpg alt="A photograph of a bicycle parked on Italian street">
                <img src=florence.jpg alt="A photograph of bridge in Florence, Italy">
                <img src=roma.jpg alt="A photograph of a ruined aqueduct outside Rome">
        </a>
</div>
```

If you want to rotate the *first and second* images and leave the photograph on top unaltered, change the following selector:

```
div#cardfan:hover img:last-child
```

to

```
div#cardfan:hover img:nth-child(2n)
```

You could also rotate the default position of the images slightly to allow the user some understanding of what is to come, as shown in Listing 3-26.

Listing 3-26. A Visually Hinted Card Fan Gallery

```
#cardfan img:first-child {
    transform: rotate(6deg);
}
#cardfan img:nth-child(2n) {
    transform: rotate(-6deg);
}
```

You could also link the photographs individually to the gallery example at the beginning of this chapter (see Listing 3-27).

Listing 3-27. A Card Fan Gallery with Individually Linked Images

```
<div id=cardfan>
<a href="gallery.html#bike">
    <img src=bike.jpg alt="A photograph of a bicycle parked on Italian street">
</a>
<a href="gallery.html#florence">
    <img src=florence.jpg alt=="A photograph of bridge in Florence, Italy">
</a>
<a href="gallery.html#aqueduct">
    <img src=roma.jpg alt="A photograph of a ruined aqueduct outside Rome">
</a>
</div>
```

However, if you link the images individually you will need to change your CSS, as the organization of your markup has changed. Rather than referencing them as children, you'll reference the images through the value of their src attribute (see Listing 3-28).

Listing 3-28. A Card Fan Gallery with Images Referenced by Their src Attribute

```
#cardfan img[src="bike.jpg"] {
    transform: rotate(6deg);
}
#cardfan img[src="roma.jpg"] {
    transform: rotate(-6deg);
}
#cardfan:hover img[src="bike.jpg"] {
    transform: rotate(24deg);
}
#cardfan:hover img[src="roma.jpg"] {
    transform: rotate(-24deg);
}
```

Note that the technique in Listing 3-26 is less flexible than creating and referencing id values for your images: if you change the filenames for any reason, you will have to change your CSS in response.

You could also raise the individual images to the foreground when hovered over (see Listing 3-29).

Listing 3-29. A Card Fan Gallery Image Raised to the Foreground

```
img[src="bike.jpg"]:hover, img[src="florence.jpg"]:hover { z-index: 2; }
```

You could have written less markup (but slightly more CSS) by using ::before and ::after pseudo-element selectors to generate the other images. (Note that you cannot use generated content on <img> tags, as they are a form of replaced element). It's also important to note that this approach practically kills accessibility, as most screen readers do not currently access generated content, nor can JavaScript gain access to it. The technique shown here is mentioned as an interesting possibility, not as a production method for central content in a site.

▓ **Note** *Replaced* elements are HTML elements that have an intrinsic width and height, without benefit of CSS; that is, any tag that produces a placeholder which then has its content replaced by an external resource. For example, when you use <input type=text>, a text box appears at a size that is suitable for single-line text input. This doesn't mean you can't apply CSS to resize it, just that the browser *replaces* instances of the <input> tag with elements of a predetermined size by default. The same happens with <img>; with no CSS, images are loaded onto the page at their natural width and height.

, <img>, <video>, <iframe>, and <object> are all replaced elements, as are <input>, <button>, and <textrarea>.

Most important, in the context of this exercise and as a general rule, *generated content cannot be applied to replaced elements.* That is, you cannot use ::before or ::after on <img> or the other tags listed above. In addition, you cannot transform inline elements unless they are also replaced elements.

Taking this route, your HTML and CSS code simplifies to what you see in Listing 3-30.

Listing 3-30. HTML and CSS Code for a Card Fan Effect with Generated Content

```
<div id=cardfan>
        <img src=florence.jpg alt="A photograph of bridge in Florence, Italy">
</div>

#cardfan { position: relative; margin: 0 auto; }
#cardfan, #cardfan img, #cardfan img:before, #cardfan img:after {
    width: 640px; height: 480px;
}
#cardfan img, #cardfan:before, #cardfan:after {
    border: 32px solid #ffe;
    box-shadow: 12px 12px 10px rgba(0, 0, 0, 0.2);
    position: absolute;
    transform-origin: center 1200px;
}
div#cardfan::before { content: url(bike.jpg); }
#cardfan::after { content: url(roma.jpg); }
#cardfan::before, div#cardfan:after { position: absolute; left: 0; top: 0; }
#cardfan::before { transform: rotate(6deg); }
#cardfan::after { transform: rotate(-6deg);  }
```

The code in Listing 3-30 creates the same card fan effect, with arguably more adaptability; to change the photographs on either side of the central image, you only need to modify your CSS, not your markup. This approach also has significant downsides, as noted previously.

You can animate these generated images by chaining pseudo-selectors, as shown in Listing 3-31.

Listing 3-31. CSS Code to Animate Generated Content

```
div#cardfan:hover::before {
    transform: rotate(24deg);
}
div#cardfan:hover::after {
    transform: rotate(-24deg);
}
```

■ **Note** Why the double colon in `::before` and `::after`? One of the few formal changes to existing selectors between CSS2 and 3 was the W3C's addition of another colon in generated content selectors, in order to distinguish their different nature. Modern browsers will recognize and support `::` or `:` prepended to generated content selectors. In this book, I've used the new formal version; for greater backward compatibility with older browsers, you may wish to use just one colon.

Clapperboard Image Captions with Different Entry and Exit Effects

While bringing in image captions from the top or bottom works for short pieces of text, the transitions can be a little large and clunky when there is a great deal of text involved. If the caption text is very long, it may be better to "swing" it in on hover.

You'll use much the same approach you used previously: an image of known dimension (supplied courtesy of NASA), using overflow: hidden to conceal the caption until you reveal it on hover (see Figure 3-8).

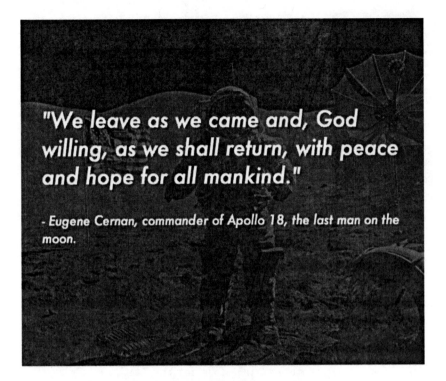

Figure 3-8. *A clapperboard caption animation*

The HTML and CSS for the clapperboard caption shown in Figure 3-8 is shown in Listing 3-32.

Listing 3-32. Code to Create a Clapperboard Caption

```
<figure class=clapperboard>
<img src=apollo-17.jpg alt="Photograph of astronaut on the Moon">
<figcaption>
<q>We leave as we came and, God willing, as we shall return, with peace and hope...</q>
- Eugene Cernan, commander of Apollo 18, the last man on the moon.
</figcaption>
</figure>

figure.clapperboard { position: relative; }
figure.clapperboard figcaption { position: absolute; top: 0; left: 0; padding: 2rem; }
figure.clapperboard, figure.clapperboard figcaption { width:618px;height:515px; }
figure.clapperboard figcaption q { font-size: 2rem; display: block; margin-bottom: 2rem; }
```

You haven't yet hidden the caption , which makes it easier to position: you will need to rotate the figcaption element 90 degrees, so that its bottom right corner matches the corner of the image (see Figure 3-9).

Figure 3-9. *Figure and Rotated Caption, with Relocated transform-origin Highlighted*

The code to position the caption in Figure 3-9 can be seen in Listing 3-33. (Note that I've used the CSS3 box-sizing property to ensure that the figcaption remains the right width and height after padding is added.)

Listing 3-33. CSS Code to Position a Clapperboard Caption

```
figure.clapperboard figcaption { font-family: Futura, Arial, sans-serif;
font-weight: 100; font-style: italic; color: black;
box-sizing: border-box;
font-size: 1.2rem; padding: 2rem; padding-top: 8rem;
border: 2px solid black;
transform-origin: bottom right; transform: rotate(90deg);
}
```

Now that the caption is in the right location, you can turn off the border, set overflow to hidden, and reverse the colors (see Listing 3-34).

Listing 3-34. CSS Code to Position a Clapperboard Caption

```
figure.clapperboard, figure.clapperboard figcaption {
    width:618px;height:515px;
    overflow: hidden;
}
figure.clapperboard figcaption {
    font-family: Futura, Arial, sans-serif;
    font-weight: 100; font-style: italic; color: white;
    font-size: 1.2rem; padding: 2rem; padding-top: 8rem;
    box-sizing: border-box;
    background: rgba(0,0,0,0);
```

```
    transform-origin: bottom right;
    transform: rotate(90deg);
}
figure.clapperboard:hover figcaption {
    transform: rotate(0);
}
```

To make this an animated transition, add the following to the `figure.clapperboard figcaption` declaration: `transition: transform 2s cubic-bezier(.12,.49,.17,.87);`.

(Note that you're restricting the transition to tracking just the transformation by using the appropriate property: this is both more efficient and makes it far easier to track the code when you return to it in six months time... while avoiding unexpected transitions just because you've changed something else between the default and rotated states of the caption).

While this works, there are still a few issues. For example, the text really isn't clear enough to be read against the spacesuit and the backdrop of the moon, so you'll want to add some `text-shadow` and `background` to the `figcaption`.

Listing 3-35. Improved Code for a Clapperboard Caption Transition

```
figure.clapperboard figcaption {
    font-family: Futura, Arial, sans-serif;
    font-weight: 100; font-style: italic; color: white;
    font-size: 1.2rem; padding: 2rem; padding-top: 8rem;
    box-sizing: border-box;
    background: rgba(0,0,0,0.6);
    text-shadow: 3px 3px 1px rgba(0,0,0,0.6);
    transform-origin: bottom right;
    transform: rotate(90deg);
    transition: transform 2s cubic-bezier(.12,.49,.17,.87);
}
```

That's a significant improvement to the legibility of the text, but the way the edge of the background comes down still looks a little odd. There are a few possible solutions: one is to make the `figcaption` wider, pushing the text to the right and the `figcaption` itself to the left, so that the box comes down in more of a visual "slicing" effect (Listing 3-36).

Listing 3-36. Improved Code for a Clapperboard Caption Transition

```
figure.clapperboard figcaption {
    width: 1236px; height:515px;
    font-family: Futura, Arial, sans-serif;
    font-weight: 100; font-style: italic; color: white;
    font-size: 1.2rem; padding:
    padding: 8rem 2rem 0 660px;
    box-sizing: border-box;
    background: rgba(0,0,0,0.6);
    text-shadow: 3px 3px 1px rgba(0,0,0,0.6);
    transform-origin: bottom right;
    transform: rotate(90deg);
    left: -618px;
    transition: transform 2s cubic-bezier(.12,.49,.17,.87);
}
```

In this case, I've made the `figcaption` twice as wide as it was before and padded the content in from the left side so that it arrives to cover the same portion of the image. By changing the position of the `figcaption` box and the location of the element's transformation origin you'll find that it is possible to create many different kinds of effects.

Creating Separate Transition Sequences

The other method for creating a caption transition is to fade in the caption background *after* the text has been rotated into place. This requires animating two separate properties, and delaying one until after the first has completed. Setting the `background` of the `figcaption` to completely transparent by default can start this process, followed by separating the transition effects with commas and adding a delay to one set of values. See Figure 3-10 for an example.

Figure 3-10. *Extended* `figcaption` *for a better clapboard caption transition effect. (overflow: hidden is turned off, colors are reversed, and a border is added for the purposes of illustration.)*

Listing 3-37 presents the full CSS code.

Listing 3-37. CSS Code for a Clapperboard Caption

```
figure.clapperboard { position: relative; overflow: hidden; }
figure.clapperboard figcaption { position: absolute; top: 0; left: 0; padding: 2rem; }
figure.clapperboard, figure.clapperboard figcaption { width:618px;height:515px; }
figure.clapperboard figcaption {
    font-family: Futura, Arial, sans-serif; font-weight: 100; font-style: italic;
    color: white;  font-size: 1.2rem; padding: 2rem; padding-top: 8rem;
    box-sizing: border-box; background: rgba(0,0,0,0);
    text-shadow: 3px 3px 1px rgba(0,0,0,0.6);
    transform-origin: bottom right; transform: rotate(90deg);
}
figure.clapperboard:hover figcaption {
    transform: rotate(0);
    opacity: 1;
    background: rgba(0,0,0,0.6);
    transition: transform 2s cubic-bezier(.12,.49,.17,.87), background .9s linear 2.2s;
}
figure.clapperboard figcaption q { font-size: 2rem; display: block; margin-bottom: 2rem; }
```

You'll notice that the background now fades in 200 milliseconds after the text rotates into place. The one remaining issue is that the caption disappears instantly when the user moves the mouse off the image, causing the same issue that you encountered when I introduced transitions in Chapter 2. Moving the transition code into the default state for figcaption will mean that the transition will reverse itself on mouseout, which will look a little odd, too. What you want, ideally, is to have the figcaption disappear in a different way than it appeared.

Changing the Exit Event

To achieve this effect, you will be animating three properties: opacity, transform, and background. You'll divide the transition explicitly into separate components to make it easier to track. The order in which you specify the properties must be the same each time for this effect to work.

First, however, you will add opacity to the various states (Listing 3-38).

Listing 3-38. Improved CSS Code for a Clapperboard Caption

```
figure.clapperboard figcaption {
    opacity: 0;
...

figure.clapperboard:hover figcaption {
    opacity: 1;
...
```

Right now this makes no difference at all, as the caption is invisible in its default state due to overflow: hidden on the figure element. But it will make a difference later, as you will soon see.

Next, you will break down the various animation components (Listing 3-39).

Listing 3-39. CSS Code for a Clapperboard Caption

```
figure.clapperboard:hover figcaption { transform: rotate(0); opacity: 1;
    transition-property:          opacity,    transform,                       background;
    transition-timing-function:    ease,          cubic-bezier(.12,.49,.17,.87), linear;
    transition-duration:                0s,              .9s,                 1s;
    transition-delay:                   0s,              0s,                  1s;
}
```

It helps to read the transition changes as columns, which is why I have added the unnecessary spaces in the code. In this case, opacity has no timing function, no duration, and no delay (meaning it takes effect instantly), whereas the background has a linear timing function, lasts for one second and has a delay of one second (meaning that it comes into effect after the text has rotated into place).

Now to the default state of the figcaption (Listing 3-40).

Listing 3-40. CSS Code for a Clapperboard Caption

```
figure.clapperboard figcaption { opacity: 0;
transition-property:            opacity,    transform,            background;
transition-timing-function;     linear,      ease,                linear;
transition-duration:              2s,         9999999s,           0s;
transition-delay:                 0s,          0s,                0s;
...
```

These effects take place during the transition *back* to the default state, setting the opacity of the figcaption back to 0 over two seconds. You might wonder why the rotation back is set to last just under 10 million seconds. The ridiculously high number is in place so that the transform back to the default orientation for the figcaption (i.e., standing on its side) effectively has an infinite duration. Visually, that means that no rotation of the text takes place at all when the user moves their mouse away from the image: the caption simply stays still and fades out.

Background Image Transitions and Animation on Page Load

To illustrate transitions on page load, you'll make an online travel guide page for New Zealand (see Figure 3-11).

New Zealand

Lorem ipsum dolor sit amet, consectetur adipisicing elit, sed do eiusmod tempor incididunt ut labore et dolore magna aliqua. Ut enim ad minim veniam, quis nostrud exercitation ullamco laboris nisi ut aliquip ex ea commodo consequat. Duis aute irure dolor in reprehenderit in voluptate velit esse cillum dolore eu fugiat nulla pariatur. Excepteur sint occaecat cupidatat non proident, sunt in culpa qui officia deserunt mollit anim id est laborum.

Fusce iaculis feugiat ornare. Phasellus pellentesque nibh ut nunc fermentum tincidunt. Praesent bibendum facilisis ullamcorper. Praesent quis mi sit amet ipsum faucibus congue. Nulla facilisi. Nulla facilisi. Integer tincidunt bibendum nisl vitae volutpat. Morbi quam massa, aliquet sed blandit ac, vehicula nec velit. Nunc at lorem ut eros condimentum tristique eget quis tortor. Donec est ligula, sagittis non molestie eu, volutpat in velit. Mauris elit dui, cursus vitae lobortis et, consequat eu mauris. Sed vulputate suscipit bibendum. Maecenas a nibh sem. Mauris odio magna, pellentesque sed egestas non, placerat id mi. Nam sollicitudin enim id libero hendrerit tempor eget eu nunc. Phasellus sodales aliquet nibh, ut dictum diam convallis facilisis. Phasellus pretium nunc elit. Cras erat urna, tristique in posuere non, venenatis ac enim. Duis scelerisque ultricies orci. Vivamus suscipit lobortis nunc.

Donec vitae risus a sapien auctor vestibulum. Lorem ipsum dolor sit amet, consectetur adipiscing elit. Etiam id metus ac libero molestie malesuada. Ut laoreet viverra placerat. Phasellus felis purus, rhoncus id scelerisque ac, feugiat vitae mauris. In sem erat, tincidunt et aliquet id, semper sit amet metus. Nulla gravida luctus iaculis. Pellentesque laoreet, tortor a suscipit fermentum, lorem orci volutpat augue, ac imperdiet metus turpis gravida nisl. Donec vehicula, elit id iaculis semper, metus lorem sagittis massa, ut ornare velit urna non neque.

Quisque in sem sit amet lectus ultricies condimentum. Ut lorem turpis, placerat in mollis vitae, fermentum sit amet arcu. Aliquam erat volutpat. Nunc orci eros, interdum id condimentum nec, tempor eget tellus. Nulla cursus neque luctus tellus tristique consectetur. Maecenas scelerisque dapibus sollicitudin. Nam sit amet dui eu tellus eleifend tincidunt quis ut elit. Morbi at nisl quis nunc tempor consectetur. Donec malesuada condimentum pharetra.

Sed eu diam a risus tempus convallis eget sed velit. Aliquam sit amet enim eu ante pretium volutpat. Maecenas ac quam at lorem porta porta. Cum sociis natoque penatibus et magnis dis parturient montes, nascetur ridiculus mus. Duis dapibus elementum erat, varius fringilla ante posuere sed. Sed dignissim neque at diam mollis ac feugiat nunc rhoncus. Aliquam ac diam ac eros tempus euismod. Donec gravida sem sit amet purus venenatis ac placerat turpis blandit. Sed lorem velit, convallis sed elementum ac, convallis a dolor. Integer porttitor volutpat pellentesque. Nam consectetur vehicula auctor. Aenean euismod posuere bibendum. Ut aliquet eleifend fringilla. Curabitur sed lectus mauris, et mattis ipsum. In vitae lacus quis nulla egestas lobortis. Etiam sed nulla elit.

Figure 3-11. Transitioned background images

When the page loads, you want several pictures to slide from one side of the page to the other. For this example, I'll use photographs by Chee Hong (`www.flickr.com/photos/chleong/6867222762/`), Andreas Beeker (`www.flickr.com/photos/kiwiwings/2148854337/sizes/l/in/photostream/`), Gordon Wrigley (`www.flickr.com/photos/tolomea/4498923741/sizes/l/in/photostream/`), and David Pursehouse (`www.flickr.com/photos/mdid/2235443912/sizes/l/in/photostream/`).

First, you'll set up your basic page, the markup for which will remain unchanged throughout this exercise (see Listing 3-41). Note that the images are offset off the left side of the page by their width (1300 pixels) plus an incremental amount, staggering them horizontally).

Listing 3-41. HTML and CSS Code for a Background Transition on Page Load

```
<div id=wrapper>
<h1>New Zealand</h1>
<p>Lorem ipsum dolor sit amet....

</div>


body { font-family: Futura; margin: 0; line-height: 200%;
background:
```

```
        url(lake-benmore-new-zealand-panorama.jpg) -1300px 200px no-repeat,
        url(lake-tekapo-new-zealand-panorama.jpg) -2000px 600px no-repeat,
        url(new-zealand-panorama.jpg) -3900px 1000px no-repeat,
        url(lindis-pass-new-zealand-panorama.jpg) -1300px 1300px no-repeat;
}
div#wrapper { width: 600px; margin: 5em auto; padding: 3em; }
```

Unfortunately there is as yet no background-opacity property in CSS; you must either fade out the images in PhotoShop before saving them, or do something else to retain the legibility of the text as the images pass underneath it. To start, add a partially transparent background-color to the div by applying background: rgba(255, 255, 255, 0.8);.

Animating the Background Images on Load

It's easiest to start an animation like this with CSS3 Keyframes (discussed in Chapter 5), but it is possible to achieve a similar effect using transitions only, by placing a pseudo-class on the body. To demonstrate this concept, you'll add a new declaration to your CSS (Listing 3-42).

Listing 3-42. CSS Code for a Background Transition on Page Load

```
body:hover {
background:
        url(lake-benmore-new-zealand-panorama.jpg) calc(100%+1300px) 200px no-repeat,
        url(lake-tekapo-new-zealand-panorama.jpg) 2400px 600px no-repeat,
        url(new-zealand-panorama.jpg) 2400px 1000px no-repeat,
        url(lindis-pass-new-zealand-panorama.jpg) 2400px 1300px no-repeat;
        transition: 70s all linear;
}
```

This sets the images off the screen to the far right, assuming that the browser window is less than 2400 pixels wide. (A reasonable assumption to make now, but dangerous long-term: a better solution will be to use CSS3 variables or calc once they are fully supported.)

There are three disadvantages to this approach: the first and most serious is that the moment the user's mouse moves outside the browser window, the images will reset to their default position off the screen to the left. You could ease this problem slightly by moving the transition code to the *default* body state, so that the transition will begin to reverse when the user's mouse moved away.

The second issue is that all of the background images must be animated together as a group; there's no way of transitioning images separately using this method.

WHAT'S CALC?

While not technically necessary in this context, I used calc in the declaration shown in Listing 3-42 as a means of demonstrating an exciting new property. calc comes achingly close to the idea of CSS3 Variables (another new CSS3 module), allowing us to specify any length value as an arithmetic expression. In the case of Listing 3-42, the calculation simply adds the width of the current element to its parent (the body) so that the image is assured to be offscreen when the page loads.

You can read more about calc at https://hacks.mozilla.org/2010/06/css3-calc/.

The last issue, not so serious, is that the background images fade suddenly when they move behind the div. There are two obvious solutions to this problem:

- Blur the left and right edges of the div by using a double box-shadow in the same color as the background of the div and a high amount of blur, as shown in Listing 3-43.

Listing 3-43. CSS Code to Blur the Transition of Background Images

```
div#wrapper { width: 600px; margin: 5em auto;
    padding: 3em;
    background: rgba(255, 255, 255, 0.8);
    box-shadow: 100px 0 100px  rgba(255, 255, 255, 0.8),
    -100px 0 100px  rgba(255, 255, 255, 0.8);
}
```

- Expand the div to cover the entire body so that everything behind it will be faded out. Set the opening declaration as shown in Listing 3-44.

Listing 3-44. CSS Code to Enforce Opacity of Background Images Across a Page

```
html, body { min-height: 100%; margin: 0; }
html, body { height: 100%; margin: 0; }
div#wrapper { width: 100%; min-height: 100%;
    padding: 3em;
    box-sizing: border-box; background: rgba(255, 255, 255, 0.8);
}
```

Creating and Animating Fake Background Images

If you desire a greater degree of control over background images, you have to fake them by exploiting the position and z-index CSS properties to force images into the background. There are two primary methods for doing so. The first of these is to create real images and force them into the background.

Rather than drawing the background images via CSS, this technique places them as images in the code, above, below, or even inside the div (Listing 3-45).

Listing 3-45. HTML and CSS Code to Create Fake Background Images for a Page

```
<img src=lake-benmore-new-zealand-panorama.jpg alt="Lake Benmore, New Zealand" id=benmore>
<img src=lake-tekapo-new-zealand-panorama.jpg alt="Lake Tekapo, New Zealand" id=tekapo>
<img src=lindis-pass-new-zealand-panorama.jpg alt="Lindis Pass, New Zealand" id=lindis>

#benmore, #tekapo, #lindis { position: absolute; z-index: -1; }
#benmore { top: 300px; left: 200px; }
#tekapo { top: 600px; left: 800px; }
#benmore, #tekapo, #lindis {
    position: absolute; z-index: -1; opacity: 0; transition: 4s linear all 2s; }
#lindis { top: 900px; left: 50px; }
```

As separate images, these elements can be animated individually, across all properties. Providing the elements with a negative z-index pushes them into the deep background. They are animated in Listing 3-46 in much the same way as they were in the earlier exercise.

Listing 3-46. Animated Fake Background Images

```
body:hover img#benmore, body:hover img#tekapo, body:hover img#lindis { opacity: 0.6;  }
```

Again, you'd typically use keyframe animation if you wanted the sequence to loop regardless of user activity.

Alternatively, you could create the same effect by using generated content. This has the advantage of requiring no extra markup, but imposes a limit of two added elements (one generated by using :before, one by using :after). As demonstrated earlier, these elements also can also be transformed, given z-index and opacity.

Summary

In this chapter you've learned how to cross-fade two images using CSS3 transitions with opacity and CSS4 cross-fade. You also created a simple image gallery—useful in many site contexts—and progressively enhanced the gallery with transitions. I've shown you how to initiate those transitions using several different pseudo-selectors (:target, :active, and :hover), each of which will be appropriate to certain presentations.

You've animated the captions for images and, within this context, displaced the axis of transformation to create "offset" rotations.

The Transitions module has several means of delaying sequences to create layered animation effects, from the straightforward (transition-delay) to hacks such as providing extremely high time values to hold transitioned elements in place effectively for eternity. You use these same techniques to create different in-and-out effects in transitioning elements, which normally simply reverse in the same animation order they came in.

Finally, you've pushed transitions into areas that most developers barely tread: the animation of generated content and moving background images on page load.

In the next chapter, I'll show you how to apply CSS3 transitions to website navigation and other user interface features.

■ ■ ■

CHAPTER 4

CSS3 Transitions for UI Elements

Another obvious role for CSS3 transitions is enhancing user interface elements within web pages: building animation into navigation, forms, and buttons, to make information on your site clearer and more engaging. In this chapter I'll take the animation principles and CSS syntax you've explored thus far and expand upon them in lessons that will make your designs more interactive, interesting, and fun.

Modern Site Navigation Markup

Before adding transitions to your site navigation it's worthwhile to take a moment and explore the markup you'll be hooking your CSS rules into. For HTML5 sites the primary navigation should be located within a <nav> element. To ensure compatibility with screen readers, you will add an ARIA navigation role to the tag, as shown in Listing 4-1.

Listing 4-1. Minimal HTML5 Site Navigation Structure

```
<nav role=navigation>
<a href=index.html>Home</a>
<a href=about.html>About Us</a>
<a href=products.html>Products</a>
</nav>
```

■ **Note** You can learn more about ARIA landmark roles for accessibility at `www.w3.org/TR/wai-aria-practices/`.

As you can see, HTML5 allows you to put a simple series of site links inside the nav element. You may find, however, that adding markup increases the semantic value of the navigation while allowing you to modify its appearance with greater flexibility. In most cases, site navigation can be treated as an unordered list; alternatively, you might want to use an ordered list if the user will be expected to read pages in a particular order.

Whichever method you choose, keyboard shortcuts should also be added for primary links via the accesskey attribute, as shown in Listing 4-2. (Note that the role attribute has moved to the unordered list.)

Listing 4-2. An Accessible Site Navigation Code Structure

```
<nav>
<ul role=navigation >
<li><a href=index.html accesskey=1>Home</a>
<li><a href=new-xyz-corp.html accesskey=2>What's New</a>
<li><a href=about-xyz-corp.html accesskey=a>About Us</a>
```

```
<li><a href=contact-xyz-corp.html accesskey=6>Contact Us / Help</a>
</ul>
</nav>
```

This is the basis of every primary navigational interface you'll build in this chapter. To save space, you won't always need to include full accessibility features, but it is very important that you use these features in your final production code.

■ **Note**   Under some circumstances and with certain combinations of CSS rules it is possible for tiny visual gaps to appear between links if they are within `<li>` elements arranged horizontally (as in Listing 4-3). While intended to preserve your code no matter how you format it—as opposed to HTML, which collapses all sequential space characters down to a single space, with carriage returns counting as one space, unless content is wrapped in `<pre>` tags—the cause for these gaps can be intensely frustrating to track down.

The issue lies not with the CSS, but with the HTML, in the form of carriage returns between each list item. While CSS solutions to this problem exist (setting `font-size: 0` on the parent element, for example, or floating the list item elements), the best option is usually to remove the carriage returns, placing all of the list items in a single line, as shown in Listing 4-3.

Listing 4-3. An Accessible Site Navigation Code Structure Without Extra Spaces

```
<nav>
<ul role=navigation><li><a href=index.html accesskey=1>Home</a><li><a href=new-xyz-↵
corp.html accesskey=2>What's New</a><li><a href=about-xyz-corp.html accesskey=a>About↵
Us</a><li><a href=contact-xyz-corp.html accesskey=6>Contact Us / Help</a></ul>
</nav>
```

For the sake of clarity I will not be using this solution in the code samples to come, but you should be aware of the potential problem and its solution.

Regardless of whether or not they are written in a single line of code, navigational structures built with ordered or unordered lists will display each link on a separate line. To create a horizontal navigation bar, you must make one addition to your CSS.

Horizontal Navigation Bar Basics

Horizontal navigation interfaces are usually employed when a site is relatively small. (Drop-down menu bars, which I will cover shortly, are an exception to this rule.)

"The magical number seven, plus or minus 2" is an effective rule of thumb to determine navigational structure: on average, human beings can recall or relate to up to seven items at any one time. More than seven items in your navigation usually means that you'll need to reconsider the UI (user interface)—*chunking* or grouping related items together usually solves the problem. Depending on screen width, you can also usually fit seven navigational items horizontally in a navigational browser window; very narrow windows (as on a mobile device) or more than seven primary links usually call for a vertically-oriented navigational format.

Links are automatically presented inline, so there's little need to add CSS just to make them look organized in a horizontal navigation bar. If you've wrapped the links in `<li>` tags, there is little work to be done: just add the declaration in Listing 4-4 to your stylesheet.

Listing 4-4. CSS to Create a Horizontal Navigation Bar from an HTML5 Navigational Structure

```
nav li { display: inline; }
```

Now that you have established the basic markup for the most common site navigation formats, you can move on to enhancing them with CSS3.

A Simple Navigation Bar Enhanced with CSS3

Let's take the simplest possible markup for navigation from Listing 1-1 and place a background-image behind the navigation bar. You'll visually format the text so that it can still be read by adding a text-shadow and a hover effect, as in Listing 4-5.

Listing 4-5. CSS to Create a Horizontal Navigation Bar from an HTML5 Navigational Structure

```
nav { background: url(images/clouds.jpg) no-repeat; padding: 1em 0; }
nav a { text-decoration: none; color: #fff; padding: 1em;
font-family: Futura, Arial, sans-serif;
text-shadow: 2px 2px 1px rgba(0, 0, 0, 0.6); }
nav a:hover { background: rgba(0, 0, 0, 0.7); }
```

Then you'll add a simple transition to fade in the background behind a hovered link over time, by adjusting the nav a selector in Listing 4-6.

Listing 4-6. Using CSS3 to Introduce a Transition Effect to a Link

```
nav a { text-decoration: none; color: #fff; padding: 1em;
font-family: Futura, Arial, sans-serif;
text-shadow: 2px 2px 1px rgba(0, 0, 0, 0.6);
-webkit-transition: background .85s ease-in-out;
-moz-transition: background .85s ease-in-out;
-o-transition: background .85s ease-in-out;
transition: background .85s ease-in-out;
 }
```

Finally, a little bit of a safety check: anytime you place an image in the background of an element you should also set a background-color that represents the primary hue of the image, just in case the picture does not load. Modifying the nav declaration as shown in Listing 4-7 ensures that the linked text will be legible under all circumstances.

Listing 4-7. Creating a CSS Background Color As a Fallback to an Image

```
nav { background: url(images/clouds.jpg) #007 no-repeat; padding: 1em 0; }
```

You can also apply a different appearance to links that the user has previously visited by using nav a:visited as a selector. As shown in Listing 4-8, you can even create a different-colored transition when hovering over such links.

Listing 4-8. Creating a Separate Effect for Visited Links

```
nav a:visited:hover {
background: #f00;
background: rgba(255, 0, 0, 0.7);
}
```

The transition effect will still be applied to visited links, but they will fade to red, not black. This will produce a menu as shown in Figure 4-1.

Figure 4-1. *A navigation bar with an animated hover effect*

Adding CSS3 in this way is entirely backwards-compatible with older browsers. If the browser does not support transitions, users will simply see a partially transparent background behind the currently hovered-over link.

■ **Tip**   The easiest way to envision the behavior of older browsers that only support CSS 2.1 is to bear in mind that they impose a duration of 0 on any transition. This, by the way, is the reason the default values of `transition-duration` and `transition property` are 0 and `all`, respectively.

If you want to ensure even greater cross-browser compatibility, you can add a fallback flat black (#000) background for the hovered links, before the rgba section of the declaration. Browsers that understand rgba will follow the last rule; those that don't will follow the hexadecimal color. The fade-in will still work and appear correctly in browsers that support it.

Highlighting the Current Page in Navigation

Highlighting the user's current page in the navigation bar is problematic. CSS is not aware of the internal state of an application—it does not know *where it is.* You can avoid this issue by creating a `class`, `data` attribute, or `id` for the self-referential link on each page with another on the body tag, allowing CSS to match the selectors, as shown in Figure 4-2.

Figure 4-2. *A navigation bar with the current location highlighted*

Begin with the code shown in Listing 4-9.

Listing 4-9. Markup for a Visual "You Are Here" Effect on Site Navigational Bars

On index.html:

```
<body id=home>
<nav role=navigation>
<a href=index.html class=home>Home</a>
<a href=about.html class=about>About Us</a>
<a href=products.html class=products>Products</a>
</nav>
```

about.html:

```
<body id=about>
<nav role=navigation>
<a href=index.html class=home>Home</a>
<a href=about.html class=about>About Us</a>
<a href=products.html class=products>Products</a>
</nav>
```

Targeting the link that represented the current page is then a simple process of grouping a series of descendant selectors, show in Listing 4-10.

Listing 4-10. CSS to Highlight Current PageLinks

```
#home nav a.home, #about nav a.about { background: rgba(0,0,212,0.6);}
```

It's also possible to achieve this effect with an embedded stylesheet on every page that addresses each link class individually. Both approaches have the same disadvantage: they require customizing the markup for each page. A better solution may be a combination of CSS and JavaScript (shown here in the form of JQuery).

The HTML returns to what you had in the beginning (Listing 4-1), and your stylesheet simply takes a new class, shown in Listing 4-11.

Listing 4-11. CSS to Highlight "You Are Here" Links via JavaScript

```
a.current { background: rgba(0,255,0,0.7); }
```

In the head of every document you include the code shown in Listing 4-12.

Listing 4-12. JavaScript to Apply a "You Are Here" Class to Site Navigation

```
<script src=//code.jquery.com/jquery.min.js></script>
<script>
$(document).ready(function(){
$('ul[role="navigation"] a').each(function() {
if (this.href === window.location.href){ $(this). addClass('current');}
});
})
</script>
```

You can use any of these approaches to highlight the current page in the more advanced navigation examples you will create in the next section.

Horizontal Tab Navigation with CSS3 Transitions

As a more advanced example of site navigation, you can include movement on "tab" navigation. In this instance, you'll put the links in an ordered list to provide more structure, as you did in Listing 4-2. You'll create the visual impression of tabs by setting the links side by side, adding a border-radius to their top-right and top-left corners and placing a gradient in the background of each, per Listing 4-13. This will produce a menu as shown in Figure 4-3.

Figure 4-3. *An animated tab navigation system*

In this example, you'll use an attribute selector to gain access to the list items and links.

Listing 4-13. CSS to Style Navigational Links As Tabs

```
ul[role=navigation] li {
display: inline; font-family: Futura, Arial, sans-serif;
text-transform: uppercase;
}
ul[role=navigation] li a {
text-decoration: none; color: #fff;
padding: 0.8rem 1.2rem 2rem 1.2rem;
border: 1px solid #777; border-radius: 5px 5px 0 0;
background: linear-gradient(to bottom, #dfc891, #776c51);
box-shadow: 0 0 15px rgba(0,0,0,0.5);
letter-spacing: 0.15rem; text-shadow: 0 1px 0 #000;
}
```

Next, you want to overlap the tabs slightly. You do that by providing a negative margin-left to each list item. The tabs will be moving up on mouseover, so you deliberately make them longer than they need to be in their normal state. Use overflow: hidden on the unordered list to hide the excess at the bottom edge, as shown in Listing 4-14.

Listing 4-14. CSS to Style Navigational Links As Tabs

```
ul[role=navigation] {
background: #000;  padding-top: 3.2rem; padding-bottom: 1rem;
overflow: hidden; margin-top: 0; }
ul[role=navigation] li {
display: inline; font-family: Futura, Arial, sans-serif;
text-transform: uppercase; margin-left: -.5rem;  }
```

The link that represents the current page will have a class of forefront applied to it. This class will bring the appropriate link on top of and slightly higher than every other tab, by using position: relative, a negative top value, and modified z-index (Listing 4-15).

Listing 4-15. Placing the Link for the Current Page on Top of the Others

```
ul[role=navigation] li a.forefront { -0.2rem; z-index: 2;}
```

You can apply this class using either of the approaches already discussed: by adding it to the markup or dynamically applying it with JavaScript. Finally, you'll raise the links on hover by raising their top position and animate the transition from the default state (Listing 4-16).

Listing 4-16. Animating the Tab Links

```
ul[role=navigation] li a {
position: relative; top: 0;
transition: 0.2s all linear;
...
}
ul[role=navigation] li a:hover,  ul[role=navigation] li a:focus {
top: -0.6rem;
}
```

Animating Custom Validation Errors for HTML5 Forms

Information entered by users into forms is usually checked at least twice: once at the front end (most commonly with JavaScript) and once at the backend (with PHP or some other server-side language). There are several advantages to this method:

- *Redundancy*: If the client-side validation process fails to work, or if it is blocked or unsupported in the browser, the back-end process will still look for errors.

- *Immediacy*: A client-side solution usually provides instant feedback as the visitor is entering information into a field or after the field loses focus; short of using AJAX or a similar technology, server-side solutions cannot provide a response until the submit button is pressed.

- *Security*: Broadly speaking, a server-side language will offer a far more appropriate and secure way of gaining credit card verification information from VISA and Mastercard than using JavaScript.

There have been many validation scripts built in JavaScript, but in HTML5 the same ability to validate forms is now natively supported in the browser with the pattern attribute and two new CSS pseudo-classes: :valid and :invalid. In order to demonstrate this you'll create the form shown in Figure 4-4.

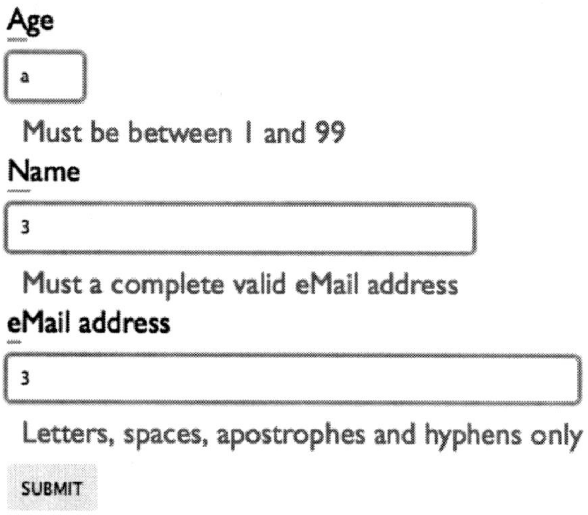

Age

a

Must be between 1 and 99

Name

3

Must a complete valid eMail address

eMail address

3

Letters, spaces, apostrophes and hyphens only

SUBMIT

Figure 4-4. *Form Error Messages Animated with CSS3*

You begin with the basic markup for an accessible form, shown in Listing 4-17.

Listing 4-17. An Accessible HTML5 Form

```
<form>
<label for=age accesskey=a>Age</label>
<input type=number name=age id=age size=3 maxlength=2 min=1 max=99 ↵
pattern="^([1-9]|[1-9][0-9]){1,2}$" required >
<label for=name accesskey=n>Name</label>
<input type=text name=name id=name size=40 maxlength=38 ↵
pattern="^[a-zA-Z]'?[- 'a-zA-Z]+$" placeholder="Your full name" required >
<label for=email accesskey=e>eMail address</label>
<input type=email name=email id=email size=50 maxlength=256 placeholder="Your contact eMail" ↵
required>
<input type=submit value=submit>
</form>
```

As you can see, you're using a number field with a min and max value to limit the user's age when they enter it, an eMail input, and a standard text input with a regular expression to get the user's name. All inputs are required. (I've added a `pattern` to the number input even though it is invalid in HTML5 in order to gain enforcement in Firefox 14 and earlier, which recognizes `pattern` but not the number attribute value itself, defaulting the field to a standard text input.) You can use some basic CSS to improve the display of these elements, as shown in Listing 4-18.

Listing 4-18. CSS for a Typical Accessible Form

```
form { font-size: 1.2rem; font-family: "Gill Sans", Arial, sans-serif; }
label,input { display: block; }
label:first-letter { border-bottom: 2px solid #bbb; }
input { border: 1px solid #bbb; padding: .4rem; border-radius: .2rem; margin: .5rem 0; }
input[type="submit"] { border: none; text-transform: uppercase; }
```

The only slightly unusual aspect of this stylesheet is the third declaration, which underlines the first letter of each form label to show the appropriate accesskey for the associated field. To display whether the information entered into the input is right or wrong, you need to add the code in Listing 4-19. (Note the first CSS declaration, which turns off the current default Firefox UA styles for valid and invalid inputs).

Listing 4-19. CSS for a Typical Accessible Form

```
input:valid, input:invalid {box-shadow: none; }
input:valid { border: 2px solid green; }
input:invalid { border: 2px solid yellow; }
```

While you could certainly animate what you have so far, there are a few drawbacks to the form as it is currently presented: the browser defaults to showing the inputs as invalid when the user first sees the page, and there's no indication of exactly *what* the user entered incorrectly.

You can't use pseudo-classes to generate error messages after the inputs because they are replaced elements, but you *can* place the error messages in the title attribute of spans *after* the inputs. Some examples are shown in Listing 4-20.

Listing 4-20. Span Elements Added As Validation Error Messages After HTML5 Form Inputs

```
<span title="Must be between 1 and 99"></span>

<span title="Must a complete valid eMail address"></span>

<span title="Letters, spaces, apostrophes and hyphens only"></span>
```

Because each span only contains information in its title attribute and has no visible content, older browsers that don't fully support CSS3 are disabled from showing any confusing messages to the user. Remove Listing 4-20 from your code and replace it with Listing 4-21.

Listing 4-21. Styling and Displaying Validation Errors

```
input + span:after { content: attr(title); color: red; margin-left: 0.6rem; opacity: 0; }
input:invalid + span:after { opacity: 1; }
```

There's an immediate problem: the browser continues to show the inputs as wrong by making the span title attribute visible the moment the page loads. The reason?

■ **Tip** An input with a required attribute is evaluated by its pattern or input type *before* the user focuses or enters any information into the field.

By removing the required attribute from the inputs and adding a transition to the error messages, as in Listing 4-22, you achieve the effect you are after. Note that I've added a delay to the transition: without this, the error message would show immediately on entering the first character in a field. You want a reasonable amount of time to pass before you start telling the user that their information is wrong.

Listing 4-22. Displaying a Form Validation Error Message After a Delay

```
input + span:after { content: attr(title); color: red; margin-left: 0.6rem; opacity: 0;
transition-property: opacity;transition-duration: 2s; transition-delay: 2s;}
```

65

You can also show the status of an input's validity by showing a tick inside the form element. Returning to the markup in Listing 4-17 and the CSS in Listing 4-18, add the CSS in Listing 4-23. (You could take this further by turning the `tick.png` into a sprite image and manipulating it to show a cross when the input is invalid).

Listing 4-23. Displaying a Background Image for Form Input Validation

```
input:focus:valid { background-image: url(tick.png); background-repeat: no-repeat;
background-position: right 6px;  }
```

You can't fade-in the background image directly (there is, as yet, no direct control for opacity on background images), but you *can* manipulate an image, so if you wanted to fade-in the symbol, you could place the image after the input and transition it as you did the earlier validation messages.

■ **Note**   You could also turn off the browser's built-in form validation messages entirely via JavaScript, as shown here, using jQuery:

```
$(document).ready(function() {
$('form').bind('invalid', function(e){

$(e.target).attr('validity')
}); });
```

UI Button Depress Transition

With CSS, you can also give the impression of a link or button lowering or sinking into the page, as shown in Figure 4-5.

Figure 4-5. A typical button example

A simple way to achieve this effect is shown in Listing 4-24.

Listing 4-24. CSS to Make a Link Lowered When Clicked

```
a:active { position: relative; top: 1px; }
```

Of course, it is also possible to more elaborately style a link, as in Listing 4-25.

Listing 4-25. HTML and CSS to Create a Giant Help Button

```
<a href=# class=bigbutton>help</a>

a.bigbutton {
font-family: "Blue Highway"; text-transform: uppercase; color: #fff;
background: radial-gradient(center 50px, circle farthest-corner, #ef6634, #c63a17 43%,#ba1a01
45%,#bf6e4e 100%);
display: inline-block; width: 200px; height: 200px; border-radius: 100%;
font-size: 70px; text-decoration: none; text-align: center; padding-top: 50px;
box-sizing: border-box; font-weight: 900;
box-shadow: 0 8px 0 rgb(183,0,0), 0 15px 20px rgba(0,0,0,.35);
text-shadow: 0 3px 1px rgba(122,17,8,.8);
transition: .4s all ease-in;
}
```

Here you create the impression of a 3D button by creating two box shadows: one to create the impression of an edge to the button, and another beneath it as a general shadow. You create the impression of the button lowering by transitioning four simultaneous actions:

1. Lower the text on the button.

2. Physically lower the entire button by using translate.

3. Reduce the shadow that represents the edge of the button.

4. Reduce and harden the blur of the shadow beneath the entire element.

You'll do this in a declaration based on the :active pseudo-selector, as shown in Listing 4-26.

Listing 4-26. HTML and CSS to Create a Giant Help Button

```
.bigbutton:active {
    padding-top: 53px;
    transform: translate(0, 4px);
    box-shadow: 0 4px 0 rgb(183,0,0), 0 8px 6px rgba(0,0,0,.45);
}
```

It's also possible to create a button reveal effect, as you'll see in the next section.

UI Button Reveal Transition

Standard HTML button elements can also be heavily customized with CSS that includes transitions. In this case, you want a button to expand on hover, revealing a promotional or guiding message inside (see Figure 4-6).

Figure 4-6. *A button in two modes, transitioned with CSS3*

Your HTML will consist of three elements: a button with two span tags inside it. You can see the markup in Listing 4-27.

Listing 4-27. HTML for a Reveal Button

```
<button>Sign up
<span class=hidden>For Free</span>
<span class=right>&#9654;
</span>
</button>
```

■ **Tip**   A Unicode character is far more adaptable and easier to control than an image when used for the right side of your UI element. I've used a decimal entity character here to represent a black rightward (A great resource for Unicode characters can be found at copypastecharacter.com.)

Next, you'll add the CSS to set up your button appearance (Listing 4-28).

Listing 4-28. Basic CSS for a Reveal Button

```
* {box-sizing: border-box;
color: #333; font-family: Futura, Arial, sans-serif;
}
button {
        font-weight: 600;
        text-shadow: 0px 1px 1px rgba(255, 255, 255, 0.3);
border-radius: 34px; height: 68px; width: 180px;
padding: 0 20px; font-size: 18px;
background: linear-gradient(to bottom, #1e5799,#7db9e8);
border: 1px solid rgba(0,0,0,0.4);
box-shadow: 0px 1px 1px rgba(255, 255, 255, 0.8) inset,
1px 1px 3px rgba(0, 0, 0, 0.2),
0px 0px 0px 4px rgba(188, 188, 188, 0.5);
text-align: left;
}
span.hidden, span.right  { color: #fff;  }
span.right { padding-left: 18px;   }
span.hidden {background: linear-gradient(to bottom, #222, #000);
display: inline-block; width: 0; margin-left: 22px;
overflow: hidden;
white-space: nowrap; padding: 22px 0;
border-left: 2px double rgba(0,0,0,0.3); }
```

Because the .hidden span is set to box-sizing: border-box, white-space: nowrap, overflow: hidden, and width: 0, you only see its border on the left side under normal conditions.

You want multiple transition events to happen at the same time and in the same motion. While you could place the transition properties inside separate declarations, it's often more efficient to place them as high in the CSS as possible.

Listing 4-29. CSS for a Button Reveal Transition

```
button { transition: .6s all ease-in-out; }
button:hover { width: 290px; color: #fff; text-shadow: none;  }
button:hover span.hidden { width: 120px; padding: 22px;  }
```

Accessible Horizontal Drop-down Navigation with CSS3 Transitions

Drop-down menus are a common navigational option for complex websites. Users are already familiar with the format in the UI on their computers, so using the same interface design on websites makes sense. See Figure 4-7 for an example.

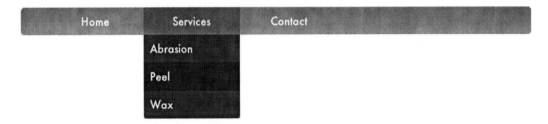

Figure 4-7. *A drop-down menu*

Drop-down menus on HTML pages have traditionally been created using Flash or JavaScript, but these tools share a significant disadvantage: menus created with them can be difficult for the disabled to use with screen readers and/or keyboards.

By using ARIA features in HTML5 markup with CSS3 transitions, you get the best of all worlds: UI elements that are accessible, visually appealing, and animated. The basic markup is shown in Listing 4-30.

■ **Tip**   You can learn a lot more about ARIA roles at www.w3.org/TR/wai-aria/roles.

Listing 4-30. HTML for an Accessible Drop-down Menu

```
<nav role=navigation aria-label="Main menu">
<ul role=menubar>
<li role=menuitem tabindex=0><a href=#>Home</a>
<li role=menuitem aria-haspopup=true tabindex=0><a href=#>Services</a>
<ul class=submenu role=menu aria-hidden=true>
<li role=menuitem tabindex=-1><a href=#>Abrasion</a>
<li role=menuitem tabindex=-1><a href=#>Peel</a>
<li role=menuitem tabindex=-1><a href=#>Wax</a>
</ul>
<li role=menuitem tabindex=0><a href=#>Contact</a>
</ul>
</nav>
```

The code resembles what you started with in Listing 4-1 (without accesskeys, which have been omitted in this example to save space). The navigation role has moved back onto the nav element, which has also gained a label describing its purpose, the assistive equivalent of a title tooltip.

Each list item has a role of menuitem, indicating that it is actionable, and a tabindex of either 0 (indicating that it can be jumped between by using the TAB key) or -1 (meaning that other controls, such as the arrow keys, must be used to focus them). Finally, the list item containing the submenu has an aria-haspopup attribute and the submenu itself has an aria-hidden attribute to indicate that it is not visible by default.

To this, you're going to add some basic CSS, shown in Listing 4-31.

Listing 4-31. Code for a CSS3 Drop-down Menu

```
body { font-family: Futura, Arial, sans-serif; }
nav { height: 41px;
background: linear-gradient(to bottom, rgb(93,146,207) 0%, rgb(79,79,181) 100%); }
nav ul { margin: 0; }
nav, ul.submenu { background: #35f; border-radius: 5px;  padding: 0;  }
nav ul li { display: block; width: 150px; text-align: center; float: left; margin: 0;
padding: 0;  }
nav li:hover { background: rgba(0,0,0,0.4); }
nav a { color: #fff; text-decoration: none; display: block; padding: 10px; }
nav ul.submenu { background: rgba(0,0,0,0.8); position: relative; border-radius: 0 0 5px 5px;
height: 0px; overflow: hidden; }
nav ul.submenu li { float: none; text-align: left; border-bottom: 1px solid rgba(0,0,0,0.3); }
```

The code in Listing 4-31 should be fairly self-explanatory: the main list items are floated side by side, with the submenu placed below and, in this case, hidden, by setting its height to 0.

The implementation of CSS3 in most current browsers requires you to set explicit measurements when transitioning an element's dimensions; neither height: 100% nor height: auto will work in this case. Additionally, you want the same transition effect to be added to multiple elements; rather than repeating yourself, you add the declaration at the top of Listing 4-32.

Listing 4-32. CSS for an Animated Drop-down Menu

```
nav ul li { transition: .3s all linear; }
nav ul li:hover ul.submenu { height: 126px;  }
```

This markup and CSS can become the basis of many interface designs. For example, with some small adjustments, vertically expanding "accordion" menus can also follow this template.

Initiating CSS3 Transition Effects After a Button Click

In most standard HTML, there's no way of recording state; that is, you can capture the action of the user's mouse over an element (:hover), pressed down (:active), and in some cases, entered within an element (:focus), but there are few immediately obvious ways of saying "if this element is clicked, do this; but if it's off, undo the action."

You do have a few options with CSS, however. The state of both the checkbox and radio elements is readable by CSS through the use of the :checked pseudo-class. By hiding the checkbox but maintaining accessibility through the use of an associated label element you can use CSS to "switch" the presentation of the page.

■ **Note**   While the techniques I'll discuss next are valid in HTML5 (which allows you to place form elements anywhere on a page), they are semantically questionable. There is a school of thought that claims that form elements should only be used within forms, and that these kinds of behaviors should be relegated exclusively to JavaScript. You should be aware of this contention before proceeding with the following techniques.

Next, I will demonstrate how to achieve the image shown in Figure 4-8.

Figure 4-8. *An image and description of Mars shown with an element clicked (image courtesy of NASA)*

Your markup will consist of a container div, a checkbox input, and an inner div containing some content, per Listing 4-33.

Listing 4-33. Checkbox Markup to Open and Close an Associated div

```
<div id=mars>
<input type=checkbox id=marstoggle>
<div class=toggle>
<img src=mars.jpg alt=Mars>
```

```
<p>Trace amounts of methane were discovered in the atmosphere of Mars in 2003... ↵
As methane is unstable, its presence indicates an active source on the planet that is ↵
continually replenishing the gas, at the rate of approximately 270 tons per year. ↵
</div>
</div>
```

You'll style the outer div and its content using the code in Listing 4-34.

Listing 4-34. div for Popup Text

```
div#mars { background: #000; color: #fff;
font-family: Futura, Arial, sans-serif;
width: 400px; padding: 1.6rem;
line-height: 175%; border-radius: 6px; }
img { display: block; margin: 0 auto; }
div#mars p { margin: 1rem; }
```

You want to hide the inner div by using a sibling selector to set its height to 0 and by hiding anything that falls outside it. At the same time you'll also set the transition using the principles of push-pull animation discussed earlier. (See Listing 4-35.)

Listing 4-35. Transition for Opening and Closing a div

```
input ~ div { overflow: hidden; height: 0; transition: .6s all cubic-bezier(0.735, -0.485, ↵
0.145, 1.625);   }
```

To complete the basic functionality of your interactive element you want to expand the inner div if the checkbox is turned on. As I mentioned, height needs to be set explicitly for elements to transition correctly in current browsers (see Listing 4-36).

Listing 4-36. div for Popup Text

```
input:checked ~ div { height: 480px; }
```

This works great here, but hiding and showing page content with a radio button will probably not work well for most designs. To get around this, you can associate a label with the input, "linking" the text of the label to the checkbox by using the for attribute. As a result, clicking the label will turn on the form element and cause your CSS to continue to respond, even if the checkbox itself is hidden (see Listing 4-37).

Listing 4-37. Complete Markup for a Checkbox-Associated div

```
<div id=mars>
<label for=marstoggle>Mars</label>
<input type=checkbox class=toggle id=marstoggle>
<div>
<img src=mars.jpg alt=Mars>
<p>Trace amounts of methane were discovered in the atmosphere of Mars in 2003...
</div>
</div>

label { display: block; text-align: center; font-size: x-large;
background: red; border-radius: 6px; padding: .2rem; }
label:hover { background: yellow; color: #000; cursor: pointer; }
input { display: none; }
```

If you are willing to disregard some issues of semantics, there are many possibilities for this checkbox control. It can even be used in menus to hold states open (for example, as a series of tabs with content underneath, or as an accordion menu).

Animating Form Elements with CSS3

It's possible to extend transitions to modify the appearance of form elements directly. A simple example would be a visual "wobble and fade-in" when information entered into a text element is incorrect, as shown in Listing 4-38 and Figure 4-9.

Listing 4-38. CSS for Simple Animated Form Elements

```
input { padding: 1rem; transition: .5s 2s all cubic-bezier(0.475, -0.600, 0.435, 1.650);    }
input:invalid { border: 3px solid red; transform: translateX(10px); }
```

Figure 4-9. *An animated, customized set of radio buttons*

With some caveats, you can extend this to radio buttons, using a technique first proposed by Simurai (http://simurai.com/). The basic markup is very simple: each radio button has the same name, meaning that each button turns the others off when clicked. One radio button is automatically on by default, as shown in Listing 4-39.

Listing 4-39. HTML for Animated Radio Buttons

```
<input type="radio" name="radiobutton" checked>
<input type="radio" name="radiobutton">
<input type="radio" name="radiobutton">
<input type="radio" name="radiobutton">
<input type="radio" name="radiobutton">
```

Next comes the CSS, shown in Listing 4-40.

Listing 4-40. CSS for Animated Radio Buttons

```
body, input { background-color: rgb(20%,20%,20%); }
input {
    appearance: none;
    margin: 10px; width: 22px; height: 22px;
    border-radius: 50%; cursor: pointer;
    vertical-align: middle;
    box-shadow: hsla(0,0%,100%,.15) 0 1px 1px, inset rgba(0,0,0,.5) 0 0 0 1px;

    background-color: rgb(20%,20%,20%);
        background-image: radial-gradient(
        hsla(0,100%,90%,1) 0%,
```

```
          hsla(0,100%,70%,1) 15%,
          hsla(0,100%,60%,.3) 28%,
          hsla(0,100%,30%,0) 70%
    );
      background-repeat: no-repeat;
      transition-property: background-position, transform;
      transition-duration: .15s, .25s;
        transition-timing-function: cubic-bezier(.8, 0, 1, 1);
      }
input:checked {
      transition-property: background-position, transform;
      transition-duration: .2s, .25s;
      transition-delay: .15s, 0s;
      transition-timing-function: cubic-bezier(0, 0, .2, 1);
    }
input:active { transform: scale(1.5); transition: transform .1s cubic-bezier(0, 0, .2, 1); }
input,input:active { background-position: 22px 0; }
input:checked { background-position: 0 0; }
input:checked ~ input, input:checked ~ input:active { background-position: -22px 0; }
```

■ **Note**   The appearance property is intended to remove all preconfigured default styles from an element or to allow elements to take on the look of other elements (for example, to style a span as a textbox). appearance was proposed for CSS3, but did not enter the spec of the UI Module, although it is being considered for future iterations of the specification. The property has prefixed support in Webkit, and partial prefixed support in Firefox. For that reason, at the time of writing this, the code shown in Listing 4-40 will work best in Chrome.

Once you get past the complexities of the hsla color gradient (great for creating different colored "tell-tale" lights) the rest of the code is simple: the radio buttons are made larger on focus, and on release the background-image of the radial gradient moves to the position of the button.

Summary

In this chapter you've looked at some of the ways CSS3 transitions can be used to enhance user interface elements, from forms to site navigation. There are an endless number of possibilities, which I will leave to your imagination and experimentation.

For all their usefulness, transitions are limited by two facts: they rely on some sort of user action to start them, and they always animate between two points or states. Moving objects in a curve is impossible with transitions, as is having them loop or run by themselves. All of those features are the purview of the CSS Animations module (which I refer to as "keyframe animations" to further distinguish them from transitions). I will be discussing that module in the next chapter.

■ ■ ■

CHAPTER 5

CSS3 Keyframe Animations

For creating simple animations of elements between two states, CSS transitions are easy to implement and use, but this simplicity comes with several significant limitations. To create more complex animations with a greater degree of control you need the CSS Animations module. I'll refer to the animations created by the CSS Animations Module as *keyframe animations* to further distinguish them from transitions.

If you are more familiar with animation tools like Flash, or come from a video or film background, the time-based, "frameless" approach that CSS keyframe animations use may seem a little confusing at first. To ensure that everyone starts with the same understanding, I'll define keyframes and tweening, then look at how they are implemented by the CSS Animations module.

Keyframes and Tweening

Modern animation has inherited the terminology and processes of traditional hand-drawn, cel-shaded animation developed by Disney and other animators in the early 20th century. After character studies, sketches, and a script were completed, animation development went something like this:

1. The major frames of a sequence were drawn by a supervising animator. (At the Disney Studios, this would probably have been one of the "Nine Old Men," master animators who created the establishing shots.) In a feature like *Dumbo*, for example, a sequence in which Dumbo tries to fly by flapping his ears might include two *keyframes*: one frame with Dumbo's ears up, the other with his ears down.

2. Confining the animation to only these two frames, however, would have made the sequence look extremely jerky (or made Dumbo appear to fly like a hummingbird). To create a smoother animation sequence, the keyframes were handed off to an "inbetweener," a lower-level animator who would draw the intermediate frames required, using the first and last keyframe as a reference. This process became known as *tweening*.

3. The complete sequence would be inked, colorized, and aligned. Played back at 24 frames per second, the transition between each drawing would appear fluid, creating a seamless animation.

Today, you are the master animator, with the browser taking the role of inbetweener. Creating a good CSS3 animation is a matter of providing the browser with complete keyframes with enough information to tween smoothly between them. The browser is obliged to make a number of assumptions when tweening. Poor animations are usually the result of not supplying the stylesheet with enough information about the elements, or making assumptions that are contrary to those built into CSS3.

■ **Note** Smooth playback of animation sequences occurs if a new frame is shown approximately every 50 milliseconds, depending on the speed of motion on the screen. Keeping true to the principles of CSS, the Animations Module does not attempt to define the playback rate or the number of frames shown per second (FPS). All CSS animation is defined by states (*to* and *from* a state) or how long a sequence takes (*time before* and *time after* a state). The rest is left up to the browser or client. You can absolutely optimize your CSS declarations to reduce the load on the browser and create a more efficient animation, but you do not create your sequences "frame-by-frame" (with the possible exception of step transitions, discussed in Chapter 3), and you cannot define a frame rate.

CSS3 Keyframe Animation Syntax

A keyframe animation always starts with an animation name which, as with an id value, must be unique. If two keyframe sequences have the same name, only the last one will be recognized. The animation sequence itself may be specified in two ways. The first of these is as a from ... to declaration, as shown in Listing 5-1.

Listing 5-1. Keyframes for a Simple Left-to-Right Animation

```
@keyframes slide {
from { left: 0; }
to {left: 100%; }
}
```

The animation can also be specified as percentage in time, shown in Listing 5-2.

Listing 5-2. Multiple Keyframes for a Complex Animation

```
@keyframes multislide {
0% { left: 20px; }
20% { right: 200px; }
80% { left: 50px; }
100% { right: 180px; }
}
```

If you do not explicitly define start or end states (from/0% or to/100%) in your animation declaration, the browser will interpolate from or to the initial or final states of the element(s). You can also create a hybrid of keywords and values in the declaration, as shown in Listing 5-3.

Listing 5-3. A Keyframe Sequence with a Mix of Keywords and Percentage Values

```
@keyframes multislide {
20% { right: 200px; }
80% { left: 50px; }
to { right: 180px; }
}
```

Because it only describes two states, the CSS Animation syntax shown in Listing 5-1 produces a result that is essentially equivalent to a transition, although the animation method still retains several advantages over a transition sequence, as you will see shortly.

Practically, the keyframe sequences can be written anywhere in your CSS, but I recommend that in most cases you keep them at the top of your stylesheet, alongside any @font-face declarations, for easy reference.

You may wish to place very long sequences at the bottom of the stylesheet (to get them out of the way) or even keep them as a separate .css file (brought into your page via @import or < link >), although this adds a separate HTTP request.

You call the CSS keyframe animation sequence by applying separate CSS properties to an element, shown in Listing 5-4.

Listing 5-4. Calling a CSS Keyframe Animation Sequence

```
#redbox {
background-color: red;
width: 100px; height: 150px;
animation-name: slide;
animation-duration: 5s;
animation-timing-function: ease-in;
}
```

As you can see, these properties (with the exception of `animation-name`), are very much like those for transitions introduced in Chapter 3, and they have much the same function. One difference is that `animation-duration` can be set to the `infinite` keyword, rather than time in seconds or milliseconds. The Animation module also has the `animation-delay` property, and adds `animation-iteration-count`, `animation-direction`, `animation-play-state` and `animation-fill-mode`.

The animation can also be called in a single `animation` shortcut property, as shown in Listing 5-5.

Listing 5-5. Calling a CSS Keyframe Animation Sequence with a Shortcut

```
#redbox { animation: slide 5s ease-in 2s; }
```

The animation values may be declared in any order, with the exception of the `duration` and `delay` values, which must be stated with `duration` first and `delay` following.

Support for Keyframe Animation in Older Browsers

Older browsers require vendor prefixes, as already discussed for transitions. This is complicated by the fact that the @keyframes declaration also needs prefixing, as shown in Listing 5-6.

Listing 5-6. Calling a CSS Keyframe Animation Sequence for Older Webkit Browsers

```
@-webkit-keyframes multislide {
0% { left: 20px; }
20% { right: 200px; }
80% { left: 50%; }
100% { right: 180px; }
}

#bluebox {
width: 100px; height: 150px;
-webkit-animation-name: multislide;
-webkit-animation-duration: 10.5s;
-webkit-animation-timing-function: ease-in-out;
-webkit-animation-delay: 200ms;
}
```

This repetition obviously builds up as you write in support for other older browser versions; some of the tools discussed in Chapter 10 can ease and automate this process.

Controlling Keyframe Animation Playback

If you try to play back the animation you have created, you'll see that the element resets to its initial state. If you want the element to stop at the final frame, you have several options.

- Set a long `animation-duration` for the element, letting it essentially take forever to get to the final frame.

- Set the `animation-direction` so that the element winds up in the same place.

- Set `animation-fill-mode` to `forwards`.

The `animation-fill-mode` is rather oddly named, but serves a particular purpose, shown in Table 5-1.

Table 5-1. *Animation fill-mode Property Values*

Fill Mode	Description
forwards	Element position ends on final frame.
backwards	Element returns to position of first frame.
both	Sets the element to the position of the first keyframe immediately on page load, regardless of the element's default location in other CSS. Only applicable if `animation-delay` has a value greater than 0.
none	Element starts and ends at initial default position provided by CSS outside of keyframes.

You can also return animation sequences using `animation-direction`, as shown in Table 5-2.

Table 5-2. *Animation-direction Property Values*

Animation Direction	Description
normal	Animation plays forward normally
alternate	Animation plays forward then reverses, returning to its initial position
reverse	Animation plays backward
alternate-reverse	Animation plays backward on the first playthrough, reverses for normal playback on the second

Blending and Chaining Keyframe Animations

Merging multiple keyframe animations is very similar to merging transitions, as shown in Listing 5-7.

Listing 5-7. Blending multiple keyframe animations on one element

```
@keyframes lefttoright {
0% { left: 0; }
100% { left: 800px; }
}

@keyframes toptobottom {
0% { top: 0; }
25% { top: 100px; }
50% { top: 0; }
75% { top: 100px; }
100% { top: 0; }
}

#box { background: red; width: 100px; height: 100px; position: absolute;
animation-name: lefttoright, toptobottom;
animation-duration: 4s, 2s;
animation-timing-function: ease-in, ease-in-out;
}
```

The plotted result of combining these two animation sequences is shown in Figure 5-1.

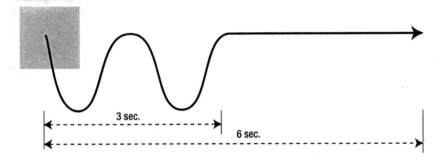

Figure 5-1. *A merged CSS3 animation*

This animation can be changed by keeping the same keyframes but altering their duration, as shown in Listing 5-8.

Listing 5-8. A Merged CSS3 Animation Altered by Changing the Keyframe Durations

```
#box { background: red; width: 100px; height: 100px; position: absolute;
animation-name: lefttoright, toptobottom;
animation-duration: 3s, 6s;
animation-timing-function: ease-in, ease-in-out;
animation-fill-mode: both;
}
```

The result is diagrammed in Figure 5-2.

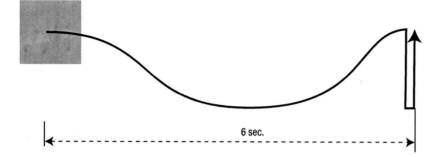

Figure 5-2. Movement of an element after changing the values of animation-duration

It is also possible to "chain" keyframe animation sequences by introducing a delay between them, shown in Listing 5-9 and Figure 5-3.

Listing 5-9. CSS3 Chained Animation Sequence

```
#box { background: red; width: 100px; height: 100px; position: absolute;
animation-name: lefttoright, toptobottom;
animation-duration: 3s, 6s;
animation-timing-function: ease-in, ease-in-out;
animation-delay: 0s, 3s;
animation-fill-mode: both;
}
```

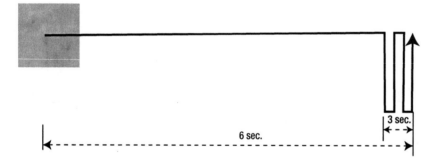

Figure 5-3. Movement of an element after setting values for animation-delay

You'll use combinations of all these features in the CSS3 Animation module to create complex animations such as the bouncing ball described in the next section, and image slideshows.

Repeating Animation Sequences

Increasing the iteration count allows your animations to repeat multiple times. An animation can be set to repeat endlessly by using the infinite keyword. For example, infinite animation could be used to create an endlessly bouncing ball (see Figure 5-4).

Figure 5-4. *Screenshots from an animated bouncing ball sequence*

To create a realistic rubber ball you need to accomplish several visual effects at the same time: as the ball contacts the theoretical surface underneath it, it should "squish" slightly before recoiling (using the principles of squash and stretch discussed in Chapter 4) while the shadow underneath it becomes more diffuse and moves further away from the point of impact as the ball rises into the air. To add extra realism, you can insert a separate easing function for certain keyframes. (This animation was derived from original work by CoDrops at `http://tympanus.net/codrops/2012/05/22/creating-an-animated-3d-bouncing-ball-with-css3/`, used with permission.) See Listing 5-10.

Listing 5-10. CSS for an Endlessly Repeating Bouncing Ball Using Squash-and-Stretch Animation Principles

```
@keyframes ballbounce {
        0% {    top: 0;
                animation-timing-function: ease-in; }
        50% {   top: 140px; height: 140px;
                animation-timing-function: ease-out;}
        55% {   top: 160px; height: 120px; border-radius: 50% / 60px;
                animation-timing-function: ease-in;}
        65% {   top: 120px; height: 140px; border-radius: 50%;
                animation-timing-function: ease-out;}
        95% {   top: 0; animation-timing-function: ease-in;}
        100% {  top: 0;animation-timing-function: ease-in;}
}

@keyframes shadowshrink {
        0% {    bottom: 0;
                margin-left: -30px;width: 60px;height: 75px;
                background: rgba(20, 20, 20, .1);
                box-shadow: 0px 0 20px 35px rgba(20,20,20,.1);
                border-radius: 30px / 40px;
                animation-timing-function: ease-in;}
```

```
        50% {bottom: 30px;
                margin-left: -10px;width: 20px;height: 5px;
                background: rgba(20, 20, 20, .3);
                box-shadow: 0px 0 20px 35px rgba(20,20,20,.3);
                border-radius: 20px / 20px;
                animation-timing-function: ease-out;}
        100% {  bottom: 0;
                margin-left: -30px;
                width: 60px;
                height: 75px;
                background: rgba(20, 20, 20, .1);
                box-shadow: 0px 0 20px 35px rgba(20,20,20,.1);
                border-radius: 30px / 40px;
                animation-timing-function: ease-in;}
}
#ball {
        width: 140px;
        height: 140px;
        border-radius: 70px;
        background: rgb(187,187,187);
        background: linear-gradient(to bottom,
                rgba(187,187,187,1) 0%,rgba(119,119,119,1) 99%);
        box-shadow: inset 0 -5px 15px rgba(255,255,255,0.4),
                inset -2px -1px 40px rgba(0,0,0,0.4), 0 0 1px #000;
        animation: ballbounce 1s infinite;
}
#shadow {top: 280px;
        width: 60px;
        height: 75px;
        box-shadow: 0px 0 20px 35px rgba(20,20,20,.1);
        border-radius: 30px / 40px;
        transform: scaleY(.3);
        animation: shadowshrink 1s infinite;}
#ball, #shadow { position: absolute; top: 0; }
#shadow { left: 65px; }
#wrapper { position: relative; width: 200px; margin: 40px auto; }

<div id=wrapper>
<div id=shadow></div>
<div id=ball></div>
</div>
```

As you can see, by merging and synchronizing multiple CSS animation sequences you can create complex, realistic motion in HTML elements.

Pausing Keyframe Animations

Animations can be paused by changing the value of the `animation-play-state` property. To the code of Listing 5-9 and 5-10, you can add the code in Listing 5-11.

Listing 5-11. Pausing a CSS3 Animation

```
#wrapper:hover #ball, #wrapper:hover #shadow  {
animation-play-state: paused;
}
```

Because the default value of `animation-play-state` is `running`, the animation will resume when the mouse moves out from hovering over the wrapper div. As you will see in the Chapter 6, it is entirely possible to set running and paused states through other means.

Summary

CSS3 Animations utilizing keyframes provide greater opportunities for animating HTML elements on web pages with far more variations than those created through Transitions. While building prefixed support for older browsers can be a somewhat arduous process, the essential syntax makes CSS3 animations much more effective and fun. While a number of the properties share commonalities with the Transitions module, the `animation-fill-mode` is very different: while elements affected by CSS3 Transitions normally returnto their initial state, it is unusual for fully-fledged animations to do so, requiring care with both `animation-direction` and `animation-fill-mode`.

In the next chapter, you'll use the syntax you learned here to create advanced animation of web content, including image slideshows.

■ ■ ■

CHAPTER 6

CSS3 Keyframe Animations for Web Content

As you saw in the previous chapter, the syntax of the CSS Animation module is more powerful than the Transitions syntax, allowing for far greater control of web content through the use of keyframes. This chapter will illustrate that power through several examples: a cycling slideshow, an image gallery that duplicates the appearance of the classic Lightbox plug-in for JavaScript, and a logo animation.

A Simple CSS3 Slideshow

Traditionally, image gallery slideshow effects were created using Flash or JavaScript, often in the form of a framework plug-in, such as Nivo Slider (http://nivo.dev7studios.com) and Camera (www.pixedelic.com/plugins/camera). While there are advantages to using a framework/plug-in approach (primarily in the variety of transitions available), there are a number of advantages in completing your slideshow in CSS3 too, as you'll see in a moment.

The HTML Code

Marking up the images for a CSS3 slideshow is a fairly straightforward process: you place the images inside a container which moves as a strip through another "window" element that is the same size as each individual image in the strip (see Figure 6-1).

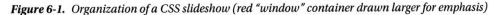

Figure 6-1. *Organization of a CSS slideshow (red "window" container drawn larger for emphasis)*

In code, this is created using Listing 6-1, to which more markup will be added in further examples,

Listing 6-1. HTML Code for a Basic CSS3 Slideshow

```
<div id=slideshow>
    <figure id=imagestrip>
        <img src=black-kite.jpg alt="Photograph of a Black kite">
        <img src=red-kite.jpg alt="Profile of a Red kite">
        <img src=pelicans.jpg alt="Pelicans on moorings at sea">
        <img src=pariah-kite.jpg alt="Photograph of Pariah kite">
    </figure>
</div>
```

In this example, you have four images at 400 pixels high by 500 pixels wide, so the total width of your inner container must be 2000 pixels. (Note that all of the images must be the exact same size; the images in the example shown are by Challiyil Eswaramangalath Pavithran Vipin, Ariful H Bhuiyan, Márcio Cabral de Moura, and Alan Saunders, licensed under Creative Commons and used with permission).

The basic CSS, shown in Listing 6-2, is similarly straightforward:

Listing 6-2. Base CSS Code for a CSS3 Slideshow Image Gallery

```
div#slideshow { position: relative; background: #000; overflow: hidden; }
figure#imagestrip, div#slideshow { box-sizing: border-box; }
div#slideshow, figure#imagestrip img { width: 500px; height: 400px; float: left; }
figure#imagestrip { position: absolute; width: 2000px; margin: 0; }
```

To create the simplest slider animation you must move the inner figure horizontally in increments of 500 pixels, with a pause after each movement to allow the viewer time to appreciate each picture. As I discussed in the previous chapter, CSS3 Animations do not work in explicit frames. You must treat the animation as a division of time: for each image you designate an equal amount of time during which it will be still with the remaining time designated for motion. In this example, each image will be still for 20% of the time, and the strip as a whole will be in motion for 20% of the time, divided into four sequences. Thus each interstitial movement will take 5% of the overall time.

The important part to remember when writing the keyframes is that properties you change *must* be present as a set value between multiple keyframes if you wish to keep them the same; otherwise, the browser will revert to interpolation using values you don't wish it to use.

Your first attempt at the keyframe declaration might look something like Listing 6-3.

Listing 6-3. Keyframes for a Simple Image Slider

```
@keyframes slider {
   0% { transform: translateX(0px); }
  20% { transform: translateX(0px); }
  25% { transform: translateX(-500px); }
  45% { transform: translateX(-500px); }
  50% { transform: translateX(-1000px); }
  70% { transform: translateX(-1000px); }
  75% { transform: translateX(-1500px); }
  95% { transform: translateX(-1500px); }
 100% { transform: translateX(-2000px); }
}
```

Then you call the animation sequence. Unlike transitions, keyframe animations do not require an initiating event, meaning that this animation will run on page load, as shown in Listing 6-4.

Listing 6-4. Keyframes for a Simple Image Slider

```
figure#imagestrip { animation: slider 10s infinite; }
```

You'll find that this works, but there's just one problem: the last movement on the end reveals an empty window, as there is no image beyond 2000 pixels for the image strip to show. You fix this by introducing a bit of a cheat, placing a copy of the first image at the end of the strip, lengthening the strip as a whole to 2500 pixels in our CSS (Listing 6-5).

Listing 6-5. Modified HTML Code for a Basic CSS3 Slideshow

```
<div id=slideshow>
    <figure id=imagestrip>
        <img src=black-kite.jpg alt="Photograph of a Black kite">
        <img src=red-kite.jpg alt="Profile of a Red kite">
        <img src=pelicans.jpg alt="Pelicans on moorings at sea">
        <img src=pariah-kite.jpg alt="Photograph of Pariah kite">
        <img src=black-kite.jpg alt="Photograph of a Black kite">
    </figure>
</div>
```

As the last keyframe now visually matches the first, this creates a complete smooth animation sequence.

A Variation with Background Images

You can create an equivalent effect using only background images—for example, to create a slideshow behind a banner element or logo. This will simplify your code to a single `<figure>`, but will complicate your CSS somewhat. (Note that you will repeat the first image at the end of the background list just as you did in the above examples, and for the same reason. See Listing 6-6.)

Listing 6-6. HTML and CSS Code for a Slider Using Background Images

```
<style>
figure#imagestrip { width: 500px; height: 400px;
background: #000; box-sizing: border-box;
 background-image: url(black-kite.jpg), url(red-kite.jpg), url(pelicans.jpg),↵
url(pariah-kite.jpg), url(black-kite.jpg);
 background-repeat: no-repeat;
 background-position-x: 0, 500px, 1000px, 1500px, 2000px;
 animation: slider 20s infinite;
}
@keyframes slider {
  0%  { background-position-x: 0, 500px, 1000px, 1500px, 2000px; }
  20% { background-position-x: 0, 500px, 1000px, 1500px, 2000px; }
  25% { background-position-x: -500px, 0px, 500px, 1000px, 1500px, 2000px; }
  45% { background-position-x: -500px, 0px, 500px, 1000px, 1500px, 2000px; }
  50% { background-position-x: -1000px, -500px, 0px, 500px, 1000px, 1500px; }
  70% { background-position-x: -1000px, -500px, 0px, 500px, 1000px, 1500px; }
  75% { background-position-x: -1500px, -1000px, -500px, 0px, 500px, 1000px; }
```

```
    95% { background-position-x: -1500px, -1000px, -500px, 0px, 500px, 1000px; }
    100% { background-position-x: -2000px, -1500px, -1000px, -500px, 0px, 500px; }
}
</style>

<figure id=imagestrip></figure>
```

You could also create a single container element with multiple background images and move it through a visible "window", or make a single image for the background that joins all of the images together. The latter approach will make the CSS easier, but will also make it substantially more difficult to change the gallery later.

Pausing the Slideshow

It's reasonable to allow the user to pause the slider to focus on one image. The easiest way to initiate such an action is a hover on the slider itself; at the same time, you should place a visual identifier on the slideshow to clearly indicate that it is in a paused state. For this example, I'll do so by fading the imagestrip element and placing a text substitute for a pause icon on the screen as a pseudo-element (I could also use an image file). All of the changes are additions to the CSS, as shown in Listing 6-7.

Listing 6-7. CSS Code to Pause an Image Gallery Slideshow on hover

```
div#slideshow:hover figure#imagestrip { animation-play-state:paused; opacity: 0.5; }
div#slideshow:hover:before {
content: "▐▐"; font-size: 200px;
color: rgba(255,255,255, 0.7);
position: absolute;
left: 160px; top: 80px;
}
```

Note that you could ease in the visual identifiers of the paused state by placing an appropriate transition on the inner figure element, such as transition: 1s opacity linear.

Altering the Transition Between Images

Ultimately there are many possible kinds of fades and wipes between each image in your slider gallery, a few of which are shown next.

Fade-In-Out

After a simple horizontal or vertical crawl, the most common transition for a slider is to have each image fade to/from black in sequence. Without altering the markup, you could fade the image strip out, move the image strip "under cover of darkness" while it is black and then fade the strip in as a whole again, as shown in Listing 6-8.

Listing 6-8. CSS Code to Pause an Image Gallery Slideshow on hover

```
@keyframes slider {
  0%  { transform: translateX(0); }
  20% { opacity: 1; }
  22% { opacity: 0; transform: translateX(0); }
```

```
    23% { opacity: 0; transform: translateX(-500px);  }
    25%,    45% { opacity: 1; }
    47% { opacity: 0; transform: translateX(-500px); }
    48% { opacity: 0; transform: translateX(-1000px); }
    50%,    70% { opacity: 1; }
    72% { opacity: 0; transform: translateX(-1000px); }
    73% { opacity: 0; transform: translateX(-1500px); }
    75%, 95%  { opacity: 1; }
    97% { opacity: 0; transform: translateX(-1500px);   }
    98% { opacity: 0; transform: translateX(-2000px); }
   100% { opacity: 1; transform: translateX(-2000px); }
}
```

Note that I'm grouping keyframes that have the same properties in the same way you would group ordinary CSS selectors. Typically, however, you'll want to make the call on the animation longer to prevent it from appearing rushed. I'd suggest using `animation: slider 20s infinite`.

Because the other images in the strip are not visible during the fade sequences, you can drop the final duplicate image on the end of the slider div, running it back to the beginning in complete darkness before starting the animation again. That will not be possible in the next example.

Fade-In-Out During Motion

You can retain the impression of a slider effect with a fade by fading the images out during their movement from left to right. While it's entirely possible to do this in a single keyframe animation, it's probably easiest to create the code as two sequences running simultaneously.

To achieve this, you revert to your original slider keyframe sequence, now running over 30 seconds, and add in a new fader keyframe declaration (see Listing 6-9).

Listing 6-9. CSS Code to Pause an Image Gallery Slideshow on hover

```
@keyframes slider {
     0%  { transform: translateX(0px); }
     20% { transform: translateX(0px); }
     25% { transform: translateX(-500px); }
     45% { transform: translateX(-500px); }
     50% { transform: translateX(-1000px); }
     70% { transform: translateX(-1000px); }
     75% { transform: translateX(-1500px); }
     95% { transform: translateX(-1500px); }
     100% { transform: translateX(-2000px); }
}
@keyframes fader {
     0% { opacity: 1; }
     70% { opacity: 1; }
     90% { opacity: 0; ease-out; }
     95% { opacity: 0; }
     100% { opacity: 1; ease-in; }
  }

figure#imagestrip { width: 2500px;
animation: slider 30s infinite, fader 7.5s infinite; }
```

The philosophy behind the timing is simple: with a total animation length of 30 seconds, each image in the slide will appear fully on-screen for 6 seconds (20% of the animation time), and move to the left in 1.5 seconds (5% of the total time). By looping a second animation that fades out the imagestrip element near the end over 7.5 seconds, you can merge the two to get a smooth result.

CrossFade

To achieve a crossfade effect you have three options, but in all cases the images are no longer placed as a "strip", but stacked one on top of the other, with the topmost image faded out in turn.

The first and easiest option is to simply set each background image as a keyframe for an otherwise empty (but correctly sized) element (see Listing 6-10).

Listing 6-10. CSS code for a crossfade image slider

```
@keyframes imageswap {
    0% { background-image: url(black-kite.jpg);   }
    20% { background-image: url(red-kite.jpg);   }
    40% { background-image: url(pelicans.jpg);   }
    80% { background-image: url(pariah-kite.jpg);   }
    100% { background-image: url(black-kite.jpg);   }
}
```

This will simply and easily crossfade between the images; however, it may not give you the results or degree of control you are after. An alternative approach is to bring the images onto the page by using the crossfade filter, as shown in Listing 6-11.

Listing 6-11. Alternative CSS Code for a Crossfade Image Slider

```
@keyframes slider {
    0%  { background-image: url(black-kite.jpg); }
    20% { background-image: cross-fade(url(black-kite.jpg), url(red-kite.jpg),0%); }
    25% { background-image: cross-fade(url(black-kite.jpg), url(red-kite.jpg),100%); }
    45% { background-image: cross-fade(url(red-kite.jpg), url(pelicans.jpg),0%); }
    50% { background-image: cross-fade(url(red-kite.jpg), url(pelicans.jpg),100%); }
    70% { background-image: cross-fade(url(pelicans.jpg), url(pariah-kite.jpg),0%); }
    75% { background-image: cross-fade(url(pelicans.jpg), url(pariah-kite.jpg),100%); }
    95% { background-image: cross-fade(url(pariah-kite.jpg), url(black-kite.jpg),0%); }
    100% { background-image: cross-fade(url(pariah-kite.jpg), url(black-kite.jpg),100%); }
}
```

The third option, using "real" images, is slightly more complex: the topmost image must be faded out, then delayed before returning to the foreground. (Think of a deck of cards, with the transition taking place between the card on top and the one underneath before the first card is placed in a discard pile for a period of time.) The CSS becomes what's shown in Listing 6-12.

Listing 6-12. Third Option CSS Code for a Crossfade Image Slider

```
@keyframes slider {
    0%, 25% { opacity: 1;   }
    30%, 100% { opacity: 0;   }
}
```

```
figure#imagestrip {
    width: 500px; height: 400px;
    background: #000; box-sizing: border-box; overflow: hidden;
    position: relative;
}
figure#imagestrip img { position: absolute; top: 0; left: 0; }
```

The HTML also changes; note that I've placed the images in *reverse* order in the new code (Listing 6-13). Positioned absolutely, the last image in the figure will be on top. (Alternatively, you could place an inline z-index property on each).

Listing 6-13. HTML Code for Third Option Crossfade Image Slider

```
<figure id=imagestrip>
<img src=black-kite.jpg alt="Photograph of a Black kite">
<img src=pariah-kite.jpg alt="Photograph of a Pariah kite" style="animation: slider 10s 7.5s
infinite;">
<img src=pelicans.jpg alt="Pelicans on moorings at sea "style="animation: slider 10s 5s
infinite;">
<img src=red-kite.jpg alt="Photograph of a Red kite" style="animation: slider 10s 2.5s
infinite;">
<img src=black-kite.jpg alt=" Photograph of a Black kite" style="animation: slider 10.1s 0s
infinite;">
</figure>
```

As each image in the keyframe sequence is "solid" for a quarter of the length of the animation, and the animation as a whole is ten seconds long, each subsequent call to the keyframe is delayed by an additional one-fourth of the total time. The extra time given to the first pass (the animation of the black kite) is provided so that the return of the photograph does not "step on" the fade into its substitute at the start of the figure.

Adding Captions

You can add captions to the slideshow in much the same way you did in the earlier examples with image transitions. The markup becomes that shown in Listing 6-14.

Listing 6-14. HTML Code for an Image Slider with Captions

```
<div id=slideshow>
  <figure id=imagestrip>
      <figure>
         <img src=black-kite.jpg alt="Black kite">
         <figcaption>Black kite</figcaption>
      </figure>
  <figure>
    <img src=red-kite.jpg alt="Red kite">
    <figcaption>Red kite</figcaption>
  </figure>
  <figure>
      <img src=pelicans.jpg alt=Pelicans>
      <figcaption>Pelicans</figcaption>
    </figure>
```

```
    <figure>
        <img src=pariah-kite.jpg alt="Pariah kite">
        <figcaption>Pariah kite</figcaption>
    </figure>
  </figure>
</div>
```

To Listing 6-2 and 6-3 you add the markup shown in Listing 6-15.

Listing 6-15. CSS Code to Add Captions to an Image Slider

```
figure#imagestrip figure figcaption {
    position: absolute; background: rgba(0,0,0,0.4);
    color: #fff; width: 500px; padding: 8px;
    font-size: 18px; top: -42px;
    transition: 1s top linear;
    }
figure#imagestrip:hover { animation-play-state:paused; }
figure#imagestrip figure:hover figcaption { top: 0; }
```

An On-Click Method for Pause

You can also use the label method discussed earlier to create an alternative method for pausing the slideshow animation by adding the code shown in Listing 6-16 just after the opening <div> together with the associated CSS.

Listing 6-16. HTML and CSS Code to Add an On-Click Pause to an Image Slider

```
<input type=checkbox id=pause><label for=pause></label>

label {
    display: block; z-index: 24; transition: 0.3s all ease-in-out;
}
input:checked ~ figure#imagestrip {
    animation-play-state:paused;
}
input#pause:checked ~ label {
    background: rgba(0,0,0,0.4);
}
input#pause:checked ~ label:before {
    content: "▋▋"; font-size: 200px;
    color: rgba(255,255,255, 0.5);
    position: relative;
    left: 160px; top: 80px;
}
```

While the above is an option, keep in mind the accessibility issues discussed earlier in the chapter if you choose to employ it.

Creating a Fallback for Older Versions of Internet Explorer

The `overflow: hidden` part of the declaration will be read and followed by Internet Explorer (IE) 9 and earlier versions, although the keyframe animation will not. This will obscure the other images, meaning that users of IE before version 10 will not see them. This can be avoided with a conditional comment that delivers the visibility of the images to those users as shown in Listing 6-17. (Note that IE 6, 7, and 8 will require JavaScript and a little more CSS in order for the browsers to recognize HTML5 elements, such as `<figure>`, discussed in Chapter 9.)

Listing 6-17. Conditional CSS to Make Images Viewable in an Earlier Versions of IE

```
<!--[if lte IE 9]>
div#slideshow { overflow: visible; }
<![endif]-->
```

A Caution Against Using Marquee Animation for Text

The `<marquee>` tag has a long and rather dismal history, going all the way back to early versions of Internet Explorer. Never a standardized element nor a part of any HTML spec, `<marquee>` was commonly used to create a scrolling "ticker tape" effect for text on web pages during the late 90s. Together with animated GIFs and blinking text, `<marquee>`, except in very specific contexts, became one of the hallmarks of bad web design.

While the naive designer might be tempted to use these techniques as a way of animating a text crawl, they should be avoided. Design trends aside, marquee text has a number of usability issues:

- The human visual system is attracted to movement and marquee text is in constant motion; a marquee feature can be extremely distracting on a page.

- For the same reason, marquee text can be very difficult to read, especially for users with visual impairment.

- Including links in marquee text makes a bad idea worse: links can be very difficult to follow and click. As marquee text moves in a loop, missing a link means that the user must wait until the next appearance of the link if they miss it the first time, which can be extremely frustrating. For that reason, any important links that appear in a marquee should also appear in a static form on the web page.

News Ticker/Notification Animation

Rather than using marquee to animate text, in this section you'll create a news ticker sequence of alerts with CSS3 Animation. Each new notification will stack at the bottom-right corner of the page, displaying for a certain amount of time before disappearing. The user should be able to click each notification for more information, and the time remaining for each panel will be shown in a progress bar. (See Figure 6-2.)

As the speaker ceased he turned to leave the apartment by the door where I was standing, but I needed to wait no longer; I had heard enough to fill my soul with dread, and stealing quietly away I returned to the courtyard by the way I had come. My plan of action was formed upon the instant, and crossing the square and the bordering avenue upon the opposite side I soon stood within the courtyard of Tal Hajus.

The brilliantly lighted apartments of the first floor told me where first to seek, and advancing to the windows I peered within. I soon discovered that my approach was not to be the easy thing I had hoped, for the rear rooms bordering the court were filled with warriors and women. I then glanced up at the stories above, discovering that the third was apparently unlighted, and so decided to make my entrance to the building from that point. It was the work of but a moment for me to reach the windows above, and soon I had drawn myself within the sheltering shadows of the unlighted third floor.

Fortunately the room I had selected was untenanted, and creeping noiselessly to the corridor beyond I discovered a light in the apartments ahead of me. Reaching what appeared to be a doorway I discovered that it was but an opening upon an immense inner chamber which towered from the first floor, two stories below me, to the dome-like roof of the building, high above my head. The floor of this great circular hall was thronged with chieftains, warriors and women, and at one end was a great raised platform upon which squatted the most hideous beast I had ever put my eyes upon. He had all the cold, hard, cruel, terrible features of the green warriors, but accentuated and debased by the animal passions to which he had given himself over for many years. There was not a mark of dignity or pride upon his bestial countenance, while his enormous bulk spread itself out upon the platform where he squatted like some huge devil fish, his six limbs accentuating the similarity in a horrible and startling manner.

But the sight that froze me with apprehension was that of Dejah Thoris and Sola standing there before him, and the fiendish leer of him as he let his great protruding eyes gloat upon the lines of her beautiful figure. She was speaking, but I could not hear what she said, nor could I make out the low grumbling of his reply. She stood there erect before him, her head high held, and even at the distance I was from them I could read the scorn of her glance upon her face as she let her haughty glance rest without sign of fear upon him. She was indeed the proud daughter of a thousand jeddaks, every inch of her dear, precious little body; so small, so frail beside the towering warriors around her, but in her majesty dwarfing

Figure 6-2. News ticker driven with CSS3

   The markup for this is fairly simple: the notifications are div elements contained in a larger div, with each progress bar as a div with a span inside it, as shown in Listing 6-18.

WHAT ABOUT THE PROGRESS ELEMENT?

HTML5 has markup for displaying the time of a process: the <progress> element. While you can style the progress element in the way you want, you cannot use CSS to modify the progress shown visually in the tag (that's JavaScript). Such a task is outside the bounds of this chapter, as we're using CSS3 for every feature where possible, so it is not an appropriate element to use in this case.

Listing 6-18. HTML for a CSS3-Driven Timed Notification System

```
<div id=breaking-news>
    <div class=notification><a href=#><span>☂</span>Rain expected</a>
    <div class=progress><span></span></div>
</div>

<div class=notification><a href=#><span>✈</span>Travel plans changed</a>
    <div class=progress><span></span></div>
</div>

<div class=notification><a href=#><span>❄</span>Light snow</a>
    <div class=progress><span></span></div>
    </div>
</div>
```

The basic CSS to style the notifications is shown in Listing 6-19.

Listing 6-19. CSS for a Notification Alert Sequence

```
div#breaking-news {
    position: fixed; bottom: -20px; right: 15%;
}
div.notification {
    position: relative; width: 275px; border-radius: 10px;
    background: linear-gradient(rgb(215,215,215), rgb(165,164,169));
    padding: 60px 20px 40px; border: 2px solid #999;
    margin-top: 10px;
    box-shadow: 3px 3px 6px rgba(0,0,0,0.1) inset, 0 0 6px 2px rgba(0,0,0,0.1);
    opacity: 0.9;
}
div.notification a {
    color: white; text-stroke: 1px solid #000;
    text-decoration: none; font-family: Futura, sans-serif; font-size: 20px;
}
div.notification a span {
    font-size: 60px; padding-right: 20px; vertical-align: middle;
}
div.progress {
    height: 5px; border-radius: 2px; border: 1px solid #999;
    margin-top: 32px; background: rgb(215,215,215);
}
div.progress span {
    background: #000; display: block; width: 0; height: 3px;
}
```

There are three animation sequences: popup, which drives each notification upwards; progress, to show the time remaining; and fade, to make each notification fade at the end. Each of these are shown in Listing 6-20.

Listing 6-20. CSS for a Notification Alert Sequence

```
@keyframes popup {
0%, 30% { height: 0; padding: 0 20px; display: none; }
}
@keyframes fade {
    100% { opacity: 0; }
}
@keyframes progress {
    100% { width: 100%; }
}
```

Note that you're taking a slightly different approach with these keyframe sequences: because the default states for the elements were already defined in Listing 6-20, you're only using the keyframes to define the *from* state (in the case of popup) or the *to* state (in the case of progress and fade). The browser will automatically tween between these values and the default embedded, inline, and linked styles as appropriate. It's only when you include values for both 0% and 100% in your @keyframes declaration that you control the entire appearance of the element (considerations of animation-fill-mode aside).

All of the notification popups share the same animation, with the exception of the delay before the animation that is initialized for each popup. Working your CSS effectively means that you should put as much similar CSS as possible in a single declaration, as shown in Listing 6-21.

Listing 6-21. Keyframe Sequences Called from a Single Shared Declaration

```
div.notification {
...
    animation-name: popup, fade;
    animation-duration: 2s, 1s;
    animation-timing-function: cubic-bezier(0.325, 0.730, 0.695, 1.650);
    animation-fill-mode: backwards, forwards;
    animation-delay: 2s, 14s;
}
```

Without any contradictory statements, every notification panel will inherit all of the styles in Listing 6-21, but animation delay is the one thing you have to change for each (see Listing 6-22).

Listing 6-22. Setting Different Animation-Delay Values for Subsequent Notification Panels

```
div.notification:nth-child(2) {
animation-delay: 6s, 18s;
}
div.notification:nth-child(3) {
animation-delay: 12s, 24s;
}
```

You take a similar approach to the progress bar for each panel (Listing 6-23).

Listing 6-23. Setting Different Animation-Delay Values for Progress Bars

```
div.progress span {
        background: #000; display: block; width: 0; height: 3px;
        animation: progress 12s 4s forwards linear;
        }
```

```
div.notification:nth-child(2) div.progress span { animation-delay: 6s; }
div.notification:nth-child(3) div.progress span { animation-delay: 12s; }
```

Naturally, in the real world hand-crafting each notification in pure CSS3 would take a great deal of effort. As you will see in Chapter 9, you can use the basis of the work here to neatly integrate with JavaScript's strengths.

A Lightbox Image Gallery Equivalent in CSS3

Lightbox is a generic term for one of the first popular modal techniques used to display gallery images: the classical Lightbox effect is a fade-out of the page followed by an expansion and fade-in of the image at the center of the page. Its popularity led to overuse on the web, with many developers simply using the defaults that came with the code because of unfamiliarity or laziness. Writing the equivalent in CSS allows the developer to easily customize the appearance of the gallery to their requirements.

First, you'll use a very similar markup (Listing 6-24) to what you used for the first gallery example in Chapter 3. This time you'll use images provided by Robert Lowe, Jon Rawlinson and Camilo Rueda López, licensed under Creative Commons (Figure 6-3).

Figure 6-3. *Large image zoomed in a CSS3-Lightbox equivalent*

Listing 6-24. HTML for a Lightbox Equivalent in CSS3

```
<body id=base>
<dl id=gallery>
    <dt><a href=#col1><img src=coliseum-at-night-small.jpeg alt="Coliseum at night"></a>
    <dd id=col1><a href=#><img src=coliseum-at-night.jpeg alt="Coliseum at Night" ></a>
    <dt><a href=#col2><img src=coliseum-forum-small.jpeg alt="Roman Coliseum and Forum"></a>
    <dd id=col2><a href=#><img src=coliseum-forum.jpeg alt="Roman Coliseum and Forum" ></a>
    <dt><a href=#col3><img src=grand-via-madrid-small.jpeg alt="Grand Via, Madrid, Portugal"></a>
    <dd id=col3><a href=#><img src=grand-via-madrid.jpeg alt="Grand Via, Madrid, Portugal" ></a>
</dl>
```

You need the dd to be the full height and width of the page *and* to center its content. To do that, you'll place CSS on the HTML element itself, so that the dd can measure itself relative to that, and use the flexbox module to center the child elements of the dd (Listing 6-25).

Listing 6-25. Base CSS for a Lightbox equivalent in CSS3

```
html { min-height: 100%; position: relative; }
body { margin: 0; height: 100%; margin-right: 2em;  }
dl#gallery { float: left; }
dl#gallery  dt { width: 150px; }
dl#gallery dd {
    margin-left: 0; background: rgba(0,0,0,0);
    position: absolute; top: 0; bottom: 0;
    width: 100%; height: 100%;
    display: box; box-pack:center; box-align:center;
    visibility: hidden;
}
dd a { background: #fff; display: block; transition: 4s all ease-in; }
```

Note that there is a potential disadvantage to this approach if the page extends significantly past the bottom of the browser window, as this CSS will cause the image to always vertically center itself against the height of the body content.

To expand and show the dd element, you'll animate the image with a keyframe sequence and fade the page by transitioning the background of the dd (Listing 6-26).

Listing 6-26. Keyframe Sequence for a Lightbox Effect

```
@keyframes blowup {
    0% { width: 0;  height: 0; opacity: 0;  }
    30% { width: 640px; height: 0; opacity: 0;  }
    60% { width: 640px; height: 480px; opacity: 0; margin: 20px; }
    100% { width: 640px; height: 480px; opacity: 1; margin: 20px; }
}
dd:target {
    visibility: visible; background: rgba(0,0,0,0.6);
    transition: 2s background linear;
}
dd:target a { box-shadow: 0 0 8px 8px rgba(0,0,0,0.3); }
dd:target a img { animation: blowup 3s forwards; }
```

By linking the content of the dd to the id for the body, a click on the image will retarget the browser and undo the animation.

Adding Captions

There are a few options for adding captions to the Lightbox CSS3 code. The first adds a minimum amount to the existing code, as span elements (Listing 6-27). The effect is shown in Figure 6-4.

Listing 6-27. Keyframe Sequence for a Lightbox Effect

```
<dl id=gallery>
<dt><a href=#col1><img src=coliseum-at-night-small.jpeg alt="Coliseum at night"></a>
<dd id=col1><a href=#><img src=coliseum-at-night.jpeg alt="Coliseum at Night">
<span>Coliseum at Night</span></a>
<dt><a href=#col2><img src=coliseum-forum-small.jpeg alt="Roman Coliseum and Forum"></a>
<dd id=col2><a href=#><img src=coliseum-forum.jpeg alt="Roman Coliseum and Forum">
<span>Roman Coliseum and Forum</span></a>
<dt><a href=#col3><img src=grand-via-madrid-small.jpeg alt="Via Grand, Madrid, Spain"></a>
<dd id=col3><a href=#><img src=grand-via-madrid.jpeg alt="Grand Via, Madrid, Portugal">
<span>Grand Via, Madrid, Portugal</span></a>
</dl>
```

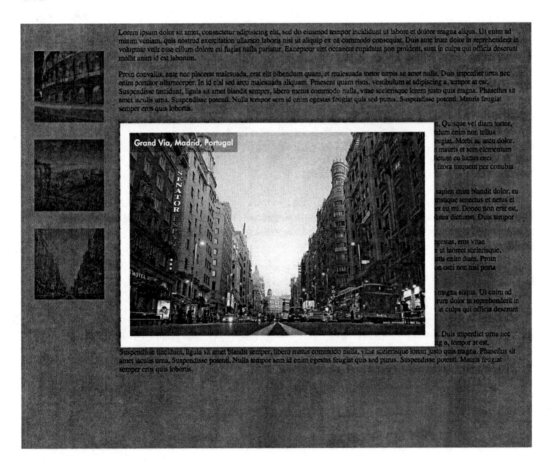

Figure 6-4. *Caption on mouseover for a large CSS Lightbox image*

By adding CSS to the dd container, making it position: relative and positioning the span absolute within it, you can transition the caption in on hover (Listing 6-28).

Listing 6-28. CSS for a Caption on a Lightbox Gallery

```
dl#gallery {
float: left; font-family: Futura, Arial, sans-serif; margin-bottom: 12em;
}
dl#gallery dd {
margin-left: 0; background: rgba(0,0,0,0);
position: absolute; top: 0; bottom: 0;
width: 100%; height: 100%;
display: box;  box-pack:center; box-align:center;
visibility: hidden;
}
dl#gallery dt { width: 150px; margin: 2em 2em 0 2em; }
dd:target { visibility: visible; background: rgba(0,0,0,0.6); transition: 2s background linear;
}
dl#gallery dd a { background: #fff; display: block; text-decoration: none; }
dl#gallery dd a span {
display: block; background-color: rgba(0,0,0,0.3); color: white;
position: absolute; top: 20px; left: 20px;
padding: 10px; opacity: 0;
transition: 1s opacity ease-in;
}
dl#gallery dd a:hover span { opacity: 1;  }
dl#gallery dd:target a img { animation: blowup 3s forwards; }
dl#gallery dd:target a {
box-shadow: 0 0 8px 8px rgba(0,0,0,0.3);
transition: 4s all ease-in;  position: relative;
}
```

CSS3 can also be used to animate a corporate logo on page load (see Figure 6-5). I'll explore this topic more when we get to responsive design (Chapter 9). It's important to play the animation only once: a looping animation will cause a great deal of viewer distraction.

Figure 6-5. *A caption added to a corporate logo on page load*

Logo Animation on Page Load

As the iris components will not be animated, only the iris as a whole, you'd normally create the logo as an image (possibly as an SVG vector file). For the purposes of illustration, we'll make it from pure CSS. (See Listing 6-29.)

Listing 6-29. HTML Markup for a Corporate Logo

```
<div id=container>
<span id=iris1></span>
<span id=iris2></span>
<span id=iris3></span>
<span id=iris4></span>
<span id=iris5></span>
<span id=iris6></span>
<span id=iris7></span>
<span id=iris8></span>
<div id=iris>
</div>
</div>
<h1>Avid <span>Laboratories</span></h1>
```

To this you can add CSS to create the iris part of the logo, and style the text (Listing 6-30).

Listing 6-30. Basic CSS for a Corporate Logo

```
div#container span {
display: block; width: 100px; border: 7px solid white;
height: 32px;
position: absolute; top: 90px; left: 90px;
background-color: #333;
transform-origin: top right; z-index: -4;
}
div#iris {
border-radius: 50%; border: 30px solid #fff;
width: 200px; height: 200px; position: relative;
}
div#container span#iris1 { transform: translate(-35px, 55px) rotate(0deg);   }
div#container span#iris2 { transform: translate(-70px, 90px) rotate(45deg); }
div#container span#iris3 { transform: translate(-130px, 70px) rotate(90deg); }
div#container span#iris4 { transform: translate(-160px, 20px) rotate(135deg); }
div#container span#iris5 { transform: translate(-145px, -35px) rotate(180deg); }
div#container span#iris6 { transform: translate(-95px, -60px) rotate(225deg); }
div#container span#iris7 { transform: translate(-45px, -45px) rotate(270deg); }
div#container span#iris8 { transform: translate( -20px, 5px) rotate(315deg); }
h1 {
font-family: "Univers LT 55"; text-transform: uppercase; font-size: 80px;
letter-spacing: 10px; position: absolute; top: 10px; left: 150px;
text-align: left; line-height: 50px;
}
```

```
h1 span {
font-family: "Univers CE 45 Light"; font-size: 25px; display: block;
letter-spacing: 20px; text-indent: 30px;
}
```

Finally, you can create the animation (Listing 6-31).

Listing 6-31. Keyframe Sequence for Corporate Logo Animation

```
@keyframes spinner {
0%   {
    transform: translate(800px,-25px) rotate(378deg); opacity: 0; }
    100% { transform: translate(2px,-25px) rotate(-56deg); opacity: 1; }
}
div#container {
    position: relative; width: 200px; height: 200px;
    animation-name: spin;
    animation-duration: 2s;
    transform: rotate(-18deg);
    animation: spinner 1.5s 2s linear both;
}
```

Note that you're not attaching the animation to any particular state, so the keyframe animation will run automatically on page load.

Summary

In this chapter you've explored uses of CSS3 Keyframes to create animations for image galleries and other page content. Keyframe sequences can include any form of complex motion that needs to be called at any time: on mouse click, page load, or another form of user interaction.

One issue that I have not addressed in animation so far is display scalability: the larger the elements in your sequences become, the harder the browser and GPU will have to work to transform, transition, and animate them. In addition, bitmap images are a big part of the total page size, slowing down connection speeds, especially on mobile devices. Neither do images respond well to scaling: doubling the DPI of the screen that your bitmap-based work is displayed on will result in image degradation.

In the next chapter, you'll look at a potential answer to all of these issues, in the form of SVG vector graphics integrated with CSS3.

CHAPTER 7

■ ■ ■

Integrating CSS3 Animations with SVG and Filters

Every browser that supports CSS Transforms, Transitions, and Animations also supports SVG (Scalable Vector Graphics), an image format that has long been neglected by most web developers. After being ignored by Internet Explorer (IE) for a decade, SVG is experiencing something of a renaissance with its support in IE9 and all other modern browsers, making it ideal for deployment in mobile development and other use cases. As you'll see in this chapter, CSS3 transitions and keyframes can integrate with SVG very well.

Filters, discussed in the second half of this chapter, are new to CSS but standardized in SVG. In fact, CSS Filters are directly derived from the SVG standard. Filters allow real-time and interactive visual editing of HTML content, particularly images, that was previously achievable only in PhotoShop. As a CSS property, filters can be easily animated, just like anything else.

An Introduction to SVG

SVG is an open, XML-based format. That fact allows SVG data to be created and altered in an ordinary text editor and in almost any web development language. SVG supports its own gradients, interactivity, text, and layers, but the most important feature for our purposes is the fact that the format describes *vector* shapes. This means that SVG images can be scaled to any size or resolution or transformed in any way without any loss in quality. The fact that the format offers a text-based description of vector information also tends to make SVG files relatively small: a simple UI (user interface) shape such as a play button, for example, can be described in SVG as three points and a fill color, rather than individually-defined pixels. This makes the format naturally responsive and a perfect fit for mobile design, high-DPI displays, and manipulation with CSS.

Consider, for example, a UI play button element. Reduced to its absolute minimum, the SVG code to describe such a shape might be something like Listing 7-1.

Listing 7-1. A Simple SVG File

```
<svg version="1.1" xmlns="http://www.w3.org/2000/svg">
<polygon points="0,0 0,400 200,200 "/>
</svg>
```

SVG data can be viewed directly in a browser. Saving the code in Listing 7-1 with the filename play.svg and loading it into a browser window gives you the visual result shown in Figure 7-1.

Figure 7-1. *An SVG play button displayed in a browser*

Note that the SVG polygon element uses points to describe shapes in a way similar to imagemaps. Ultimately, SVG elements must be rendered as pixels by your display, and by default the points specified for the polygon will map to pixels on the screen. (Your play button will be displayed in the browser as 400 pixels high and two hundred pixels wide by default, and will be positioned in the extreme top-left corner of the screen.) Ultimately, the final rendered dimensions of an SVG element are arbitrary: the button could be rendered a mile high (if your screen was large enough) or two centimeters wide (for example, on a printed page) and, all other factors aside, the quality would be the same.

Again, as with imagemaps, it's usually not very efficient to write all of your code by hand for SVG. For many tasks you'll find it considerably easier to use a drawing application and export the result as an SVG file. (I'll discuss these tools shortly.)

Placing SVG on a Web Page

There are three primary methods used to place an SVG file on an HTML page: referenced as an image, inline on your page (also called *embedded* SVG), and referenced as an object.

SVG As an Inline Image

The method for placing an SVG element into a web page most familiar to web developers is to use the <img> tag. Before you do so, your SVG code must contain a little more information as to its "natural" size (again, keeping the code to an absolute minimum), as shown in Listing 7-2.

Listing 7-2. SVG Code Prepared for Insertion on a Web Page As an Image

```
<svg version="1.1" xmlns="http://www.w3.org/2000/svg" viewBox="0 0 400 400">
<polygon points="0,0 0,400 200,200 " fill="rgba(90,70,80,0.5)" />
</svg>
```

The viewBox attribute specifies a "canvas" of 400 by 400 pixels. With no width or height specified for the image element in the CSS, the SVG element reserves a "space" of 400 × 400 pixels for itself when it is placed on your page as an image with standard HTML, shown in Listing 7-3.

Listing 7-3. An SVG Element Inserted on a Web Page As an Image

```
<img src=svg/play.svg alt=Play>
```

You can also reference SVG as an image anywhere you would normally use an image in your CSS—for example, as a background for an element (Listing 7-4).

Listing 7-4. SVG Applied As a Background Image in CSS

```
h1 { background: url(svg/wave.svg); }
```

While referencing an external SVG file in this way is the simplest and most common method, it does carry several drawbacks:

- The SVG file is treated solely as an image; any interactivity or scripts written within the code are ignored.

- You can't "reach inside" the SVG code to directly alter the appearance of elements using CSS with the same degree of freedom you have with inline SVG.

Inline SVG

If you embed SVG data directly on your page, you need to include a little more information to the SVG code. You will need to provide the element's width and height either as attributes (viewBox, width, or height attributes) or as a style (see Listing 7-5).

Listing 7-5. SVG Applied Inline with HTML

```
<!DOCTYPE html>
<html lang=en>
<head>
<meta charset=utf-8>
<title>SVG Embedded File Example</title>
</head>
<body>
<h1>Standard content</h1>
<svg version="1.1" xmlns="http://www.w3.org/2000/svg" style="width: 200px; height: 400px">
<polygon points="0,0 0,400 200,200"  />
</svg>
</body>
</html>
```

Inline SVG saves an extra HTTP request, making it particularly important for mobile pages, where lag is prevalent. Other advantages over simply referencing the file as an image are the ability to directly influence the appearance of SVG with CSS. Scripted interactivity with the SVG is also supported.

The primary drawback to inline SVG is the simple fact that it adds more code to your HTML page.

SVG Added As an Object or iframe

Adding SVG to a web page as an object or iframe is the oldest method, in which scripted interactivity is retained inside the element (Listing 7-6).

Listing 7-6. SVG Applied As an Object or iframe to a Web Page

```
<object type="image/svg+xml" data="icon.svg">
Warning for older browsers, or alternative content
</object>

<iframe src="icon.svg">
Warning for older browsers, or alternative content
</iframe>
```

However, applied as an <object> or <embed> tag, the ability to customize the appearance of the SVG elements is minimized . The <object> or <embed> tag may also appear with scrollbars if the SVG content overflows its container.

Manipulating SVG with CSS

Just as you can place SVG on a web page in several different ways, so you can manipulate the appearance of an SVG element using several different methods. This is made more complex by the fact that SVG has its own native syntax for achieving some visual effects.

At the simplest level, you can resize an SVG element when it is placed on your page as an image, as shown in Listing 7-7.

Listing 7-7. Inline CSS Used to Resize an SVG Element

```
<img src=play.svg alt=Play style="width: 50px; height: 50px">
```

You can also alter the appearance of the element from an embedded or linked style sheet, in the same way that you write presentational rules for any other kind of image. (For this reason, SVG elements used on a page are often given an id attribute.)

You can change the fill color of an SVG shape natively inside the SVG file, using fill (see Listing 7-8). (Note that fill can take any color value used in CSS: keyword, hexadecimal, rgb, or hsl).

Listing 7-8. Fill Attribute Used to Color an SVG Polygon Element

```
<polygon points="0,0 0,400 200,200 " fill="red" />
```

You can also change the fill color using an embedded stylesheet in the SVG file (Listing 7-9).

Listing 7-9. Modifying the Appearance of an SVG Element with an Embedded Stylesheet

```
<svg version="1.1" xmlns="http://www.w3.org/2000/svg" viewBox="0 0 400 400">
<style type="text/css">
polygon { fill: blue; }
</style>
<polygon points="0,0 0,400 200,200" />
</svg>
```

Finally, you can also accomplish this via your CSS, if the SVG file is embedded directly in your page (Listing 7-10).

Listing 7-10. Modifying the Appearance of an Inline SVG Element with an Embedded Stylesheet

```
<!DOCTYPE html>
<html lang=en>
<head>
<meta charset=utf-8>
<title>SVG Embedded File Example</title>
<style>
polygon { fill: red; stroke: black; stroke-width: 9px;  }
</style>
</head>
<body>
<svg version="1.1" xmlns="http://www.w3.org/2000/svg" style="width: 200px; height: 400px">
<polygon points="10,19 10,390 190,200"  />
</svg>
</body>
</html>
```

Note that this does not mean that you somehow magically have new stroke or fill properties for any HTML element, much as you might wish it. These properties are very specifically applied to SVG content only.

You can also detect hover on SVG elements, and change the appearance of the SVG content in response (Listing 7-11).

Listing 7-11. CSS Hover Detection on an SVG Element

```
polygon { fill: red; stroke: black; stroke-width: 9px;  }
polygon:hover { fill: black; }
```

Note one small but significant advantage to using inline SVG for the button: the "hot spot" area for hover is exactly the shape of the polygon. On a standard bitmap image, the area is always rectangular, no matter how the shape of the image might appear.

This means that you can also transition these effects, as you can with any other element influenced by CSS. To make the CSS clearer and more specific, I've added an id to the polygon element and addressed it that way in my styles, as shown in Listing 7-12. (Note that I've also brought the polygon "in" a little from the edges, as stroke is added to the outside of the shape, in the same way that CSS border is to HTML elements. Without this, the tips of the stroke would be cut off by the edges of the SVG "canvas" as it extended beyond them).

Listing 7-12. CSS Transition on an SVG Element

```
<!DOCTYPE html>
<html lang=en>
<head>
<meta charset=utf-8>
<title>SVG Embedded File Example</title>
<style>
#play { fill: red; stroke: black; stroke-width: 9px;  transition: 1s all linear; }
#play:hover { fill: black; stroke: black; stroke-width: 9px;  }
</style>
</head>
```

```
<body>
<svg version="1.1" xmlns="http://www.w3.org/2000/svg" style="width: 200px; height: 400px">
<polygon id="play" points="10,19 10,390 190,200"  />
</svg>
</body>
</html>
```

Any CSS3 transform, transition, or animation that can be applied to an HTML element can also be applied to SVG, making the combination of vector shapes and CSS extremely powerful.

An Animated SVG Imagemap

In this exercise, you'll use SVG to duplicate the functionality of an HTML imagemap UI, but you'll add several evolutionary steps: sections of your SVG "imagemap" will mask image content that will be transitioned in with CSS3 on hover over the appropriate areas (see Figure 7-2).

Figure 7-2. An SVG imagemap

First, you need an SVG drawing. Thankfully, there is a great deal of free SVG content available online: in this case, I will use a map of Canada supplied by Wikimedia Commons. For the purpose of illustration, I've edited the map down to just the provinces of British Columbia, Alberta and Saskatchewan.

Each province is demarked by a path, supplied as a string of coordinates. We'll start with inlining the SVG in our page and creating a simple hover effect on each path. The result will look something like Listing 7-13.

Listing 7-13. Simple Highlight on an SVG Imagemap

```
<!DOCTYPE html>
<html lang=en>
<head>
<meta charset=utf-8>
<title>SVG Embedded File Example</title>
<style>
path { fill: #fdfdfd; }
path:hover { fill: red; }
</style>
</head>
<body>
<svg version="1.1"  xmlns:svg=http://www.w3.org/2000/svg
xmlns="http://www.w3.org/2000/svg" xmlns:xlink="http://www.w3.org/1999/xlink" x="0px" y="0px"
width="1000px" height="600px" viewBox="0 0 1000 660">
<path id="alberta" d="M1654.393,678.219 ...>
<path id="british-columbia" d="M982.854,27.912l150.51,33.221c17....>
...
</svg>
```

To achieve the mask effect, you're going to embed each "show through" image after each path, and then turn the path into a clipPath. You'll associate the elements together by referencing the id of the appropriate clipping path for the image and group the elements together with <g>.

The beginning code for the SVG image, including the path for Alberta, will look something like Listing 7-14.

Listing 7-14. SVG Clipping Path for an Image

```
<g>
<clipPath id="ab-clipper">
    <path fill="#D3D3D3" d="M1654.393,678.219 ...>
</clipPath>
<image clip-path="url(#ab-clipper)" height="100%" width="100%" x="800" y="50"
xlink:href="lake-louise.jpeg" preserveAspectRatio="xMidYMin slice" />
</g>
```

clipPath defines the path within it to act as a mask for the elements that reference the clipPath id, as the lake-loise.jpeg image does. The image element is cross-linked to a bitmap picture in the same location as the map. The image is set to its full "natural" width and height and moved on the x and y axis until it is in the same location as the path. (It's likely that you'll need to set the link to the clipping path as the last action you take with the image; otherwise, you'll be playing a guessing game as to the position of the image while it is masked and likely invisible).

So now you have created a masked bitmap image. The CSS to reveal this portion of the map (Listing 7-15) is simple.

Listing 7-15. CSS to Show a Clipped Image on Hover in an SVG Element

```
svg image { opacity: 0; transition: 400ms opacity ease; }
svg image:hover { opacity: 1; }
```

There's just one problem: the clipping path is invisible, which means that there is an Alberta-sized gap in your map. The hover effect works, but the user won't see where to move their mouse if you apply the same effect to the other province paths. Once it is turned into a clip, the fill on the path is useless. You can change the color all day, and never see any difference.

109

The solution is to place a filled copy of the path *between* the clipping path and the image in the code, as shown in Listing 7-16.

Listing 7-16. A clipped Area Made Visible in SVG with the Addition of a Copied Filled Path

```
<g>
<clipPath id="ab-clipper">
        <path fill="#D3D3D3" d="M1654.393,678.219 ...>
</clipPath>
<path fill="#FF0000" d="M1654.393,678.219... />
<image clip-path="url(#ab-clipper)" height="100%" width="100%" x="800" y="50"
xlink:href="wheat.jpeg" preserveAspectRatio="xMidYMin slice" />
</g>
```

The bitmap image (by Kenny Louie, licensed under Creative Commons: http://flickr.com/photos/kwl/3102355428) is still invisible, but it is rendered "above" the copied path, so it still shows when the user hovers their mouse over the area filled with the copied path.

The final step is linking each of the areas in the SVG image. The link goes inside each group in the SVG file itself and requires use of the xlink namespace (Listing 7-17).

Listing 7-17. A Linked Clipped Image in SVG

```
<g>
<a xlink:href=" http://www.hellobc.com/">
<clipPath id="bc-clipper">
    <path d=" M982.854,27.912l150.51,33.221c17....>
</clipPath>
<path id="british-columbia" d="M982.854,27.912l150.51,33.221c17....>
<image clip-path="url(#bc-clipper)" height="100%" width="100%" x="80" y="50"
xlink:href="false-creek.jpeg" preserveAspectRatio="xMidYMin slice" />
</a>
</g>
```

Note that the area of the link follows the edge of the path, just as real imagemaps do, and the transition happens within the same area.

SVG Snowflake Animation

The scalability of vector shapes means that you can use multiple copies of an SVG element at different sizes without worrying about image quality. I'll demonstrate this by animating vector snowflakes for a seasonal background scene. (For this, I'll use a slightly modified SVG snowflake downloaded from Wikimedia Commons at http://upload.wikimedia.org/wikipedia/commons/5/50/Snow_flake.svg. See Figure 7-3.)

Figure 7-3. *Still from an SVG falling snowflake animation*

First, you're going to place the snowflake onto the page as multiple images. The flakes will be different sizes and will start in different locations, but they will share the same animation characteristics: they will fall down from the sky, drifting laterally in the breeze as they do so. (See Listing 7-18.)

Listing 7-18. SVG Snowflakes Placed As Images on a Page

```
<img src="snowflake.svg" alt="" class="flake" style="top: -50px" >
<img src="snowflake.svg" alt="" class="flake" style="left: 200px; width: 60px;
height: 60px; top: -120px;" >
<img src="snowflake.svg" alt="" class="flake" style="left: 640px; width: 120px; height: 120px;
top: -400px;" >
```

Next, you'll apply the CSS to create the impression of a winter sky through a gradient and create a base size for the snowflakes. At the same time, you'll call on two keyframe sequences: one to spin the snowflakes as they fall toward the bottom (called snow) and another to drift the snowflakes from side to side (drift). (See Listing 7-19.)

Listing 7-19. Base CSS for a Snowflake Animation

```
html { min-height: 100%; }
body { height: 100%; background: linear-gradient(#b5d3ff, #30509a); }
img.flake { width: 150px; height: 150px; position: relative;
animation: snow 8s linear infinite forwards,
drift 12s ease-in-out forwards infinite; }
```

The keyframe sequences run at different lengths, and each snowflake starts at a different height (Listing 7-20); the combination creates the impression of random cycled motion.

Listing 7-20. Keyframe Sequences for a Snowflake Animation

```
@keyframes snow {
    100% { top: 700px; transform: rotate(2.2turn);  }
}

@keyframes drift {
    0% { left: -5px; }
    25% { left: 55px; }
    55% { left: -15px; }
    100% { left: 0px; }
}
```

This works, but as you can see, there are two issues. The first is that, to add more snowflakes, you need to add more images to the markup, which quickly becomes tiring. The second issue is the fact that smaller snowflakes will be interpreted as being farther away, and so should take longer to fall off the bottom of the screen (which, for this example, let's assume is 700 pixels high). You can call on the snowflakes through the use of added classes with different timings for the motion, shown in Listing 7-21.

Listing 7-21. Slowing Animation by Creating Secondary Classes

```
img.flake { width: 150px; height: 150px; position: relative;
    animation: snow 8s linear infinite forwards,
    drift 12s ease-in-out forwards infinite;
}
img.slow {
    animation: snow 16s linear infinite forwards,
    drift 24s ease-in-out forwards infinite;
}
```

Separate classes means that a slower snowflake could be controlled by calling on two classes. Creating more variation would mean creating more classes, which returns to the same problem as with adding more snowflakes. You'll address this issue when you start integrating JavaScript with CSS3 animations in Chapter 9.

Tools for SVG

Right now one of the biggest obstacles to widespread use of SVG is the relative paucity of design tools. The most popular include:

- Adobe Illustrator has an SVG export option but, as with many WYSIWYG tools, the code it creates is not terribly efficient: generated SVG files usually contain far more code than is necessary.

- Inkscape (http://inkscape.org/), the open source alternative, shares the same issue as Adobe Illustrator. Inkscape does, however, have the advantage of working with native SVG files and it supports SVG filters.

- Raphaël is a small JavaScript library that enables easy SVG creation and manipulation from within JavaScript.

Introduction to CSS3 Filters

CSS Filters allow the processing of web content before it appears on the page. Most commonly (but by no means exclusively), these filters are applied to bitmap images. Filters significantly alter the typical web development image production workflow: rather than permanently "baking in" visual effects in the pixels of an image, designers can optimize and export an image from PhotoShop that will remain relatively untouched, leaving visual changes to CSS.

This means that images can be altered on the fly in CSS, rather than having to re-edit originals in PhotoShop, export them, and then re-upload them to a server. It also means that these effects can be animated.

Black and White/Grayscale Filter Transition

The grayscale filter effect is ideal for online portfolios or photographic galleries. Rather than using complex JavaScript or Flash solutions, a CSS filter can easily convert a color image to black and white. You can undo this conversion on hover, and attach a transition to ease between the two states, as with the image shown in Figure 7-4 (by Andrew Larsen at www.flickr.com/photos/papalars/4013594219, licensed under Creative Commons). See Listing 7-22.

Figure 7-4. *A color image (right) filtered with CSS (left)*

Listing 7-22. Applying a Grayscale Filter Transition

```
img { border: 20px solid #fff; box-shadow: 10px 10px 8px rgba(0,0,0,0.3); }
img.bw { filter: grayscale(1); transition: 1s filter linear; }
img.bw:hover { filter: grayscale(0); }

<img src=lake-louise.jpg alt="Lake Louise, Alberta, Canada" class=bw>
```

As with the other filters I'll describe in this chapter, the grayscale filter takes values between 0 (no effect) and 1 (full effect) with floating point values between. Note that you cannot transition smoothly to a state of "none" or no filter applied; the filter must be given a fresh value.

Sepia Filter Transition

The sepia filter can be used to create an "aged" photo effect, as shown in Figure 7-5 (applied to a photograph by Robb North, www.flickr.com/photos/robbn1/3650713106).

Figure 7-5. *A color image (right) filtered with CSS (left)*

The code to achieve the effect shown Figure 7-5 is very similar to grayscale (see Listing 7-23).

Listing 7-23. CSS to Transition a Sepia Filter on an Image

```
img { border: 20px solid #fff; box-shadow: 10px 10px 8px rgba(0,0,0,0.3); }
img.old { filter: sepia(1); transition: 1s filter linear; }
img.old:hover { filter: sepia(0); }

<img src=barn.jpg alt="Old barn" class=old>
```

While the barn photograph in Figure 7-5 had previously been processed in an image editor to add "weathering" and a partial vignette appearance, you've only used CSS to provide a sepia tone to the image. The other effects can also be added with CSS.

Developing Polaroid Photo Effect

It's possible to combine both a filter and a box-shadow with an inset value to re-create the appearance of a developing Polaroid photograph by surrounding an image with a div and animating the style applied to the container element. The image held inside it will need to be "pushed back" by using z-index so that the inset inner shadow of the div overlays it (see Listing 7-24).

Listing 7-24. CSS to Transition an Image with a Polaroid Effect

```
div.polaroid { float: left; border: 25px solid #f3f4e3; border-bottom-width: 45px;
box-shadow: 0 0 200px 200px rgba(29,25,4,1) inset;
filter: sepia(.8);  transition: 3s all ease-in;  }
div.polaroid img { position: relative; z-index: -1; }
div.polaroid:hover { filter: sepia(.2); box-shadow: 0 0 50px 0 rgba(29,25,4,0.2) inset }

<div class="polaroid"><img src="barn.jpg" alt="Photograph of an old barn"></a>
```

Blur Filter Transition

Blur filters need to be used carefully; applying them excessively can make a website difficult to read or interact with. Blur is one of the few filters that does not take a value between 0 and 1. Instead, it uses a length measurement to set the blur amount. (See Figure 7-6, which uses another Creative Commons image by Louise Docker, `www.flickr.com/photos/aussiegall/6311469113`.)

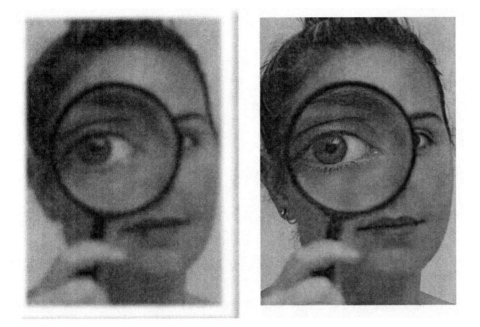

Figure 7-6. *A color image (right) filtered with CSS blur (left)*

Note that the blur effect extends all the way through the image, including the border and shadow. It is possible to limit the extent of the blur by making the border and shadow the properties of a second, parent element, such as a `div`. (See Listing 7-25.)

Listing 7-25. CSS to Apply a Blur Filter to an Image

```
img { border: 20px solid #fff; box-shadow: 10px 10px 8px rgba(0,0,0,0.3); }
img.old { filter: blur(2px); transition: 1s filter linear; }
img.old:hover { filter: blur(0px); }
```

Summary

SVG and filters are two of the most powerful features you can add to CSS animations. SVG allows resolution-free transitions and animations, while filters allow fast client-side visual image processing.

SVG is a dozen years old; CSS filters are brand new. Both are immediately limited by the fact that what you create with them is unitary: your creations can't immediately be repeated. Animating one element on a screen is easy, and you can reuse that animation to animate another element, but each new element must be created separately.

You can use JavaScript to simplify, empower, and vary your CSS3 Animations and Transitions, easily replicating animated elements and making new animations with a power that you'll explore in the next chapter.

CHAPTER 8

■ ■ ■

Integrating CSS3 Animation with Responsive Web Design and JavaScript

Now it's time to bring all the elements you've looked at so far together on your web pages. To do this you will integrate CSS3 Transforms, Transitions, and Animations with current site development principles, including Responsive Web Design (RWD).

At a basic level, a responsive site will consist of a fluid design, with most elements measured in percentages, rem, em, vh, or vw units, rather than pixels, combined with a series of CSS *breakpoints* defined in CSS media queries. The position of these breakpoints is usually defined by the values at which the page design "breaks" when the width of the browser (more correctly referred to as a *viewport*) changes. For convenience, these values are usually measured in pixels, although there are good arguments for measuring in rems or ems to break away as much as possible from the concept of "screen sizes."

Designing a site with responsive web design principles allows visitors to have a smooth, continuous, and uninterrupted experience with every device they use to access it: desktop browser, tablet, mobile phone, and devices yet to come.

It's a good practice to designate breakpoints at the widths where your design fails, rather than use the set display dimensions of the latest iPhone or iPad model. Mobile devices change rapidly, and there is much more variety in smartphone and tablet dimensions, particularly in the Android market, than most people realize. It's far better to have the site respond to dimensions that are relevant to your design, rather than the arbitrary resolutions of this year's technology.

At each breakpoint, you specify changes in layout: elements are resized or repositioned, and appear or disappear. A *mobile first* philosophy reverses the typical development process: from its inception you design a site for small screens (with a horizontal resolution of 320 pixels or less) and adapt the page as the viewport widens, allowing the site more room to "breathe." Mobile first has the advantage of enabling you to concentrate development on features that the site absolutely needs, given the severely restricted space and bandwidth of most mobile devices.

■ **Note** As a rule, mobile users should have exactly the same access to the tools, navigation, and features of a website as they would when using the site with a desktop browser. Before dropping a feature for mobile users in a responsive site, consider whether the component is needed at all.

Many web developers think of responsive web design purely in terms of `@media` queries. While queries are a very important component, and will be the focus here, it's important to understand that many responsive solutions will require additional contributions from JavaScript and server-side solutions such as PHP (typically referred to as *RESS: Responsive Design + Server-Side Components*).

What I will concentrate on in this chapter is the use of CSS animations to ease the transition between breakpoints in a responsive page. It should be noted that while designers *love* this stuff —you'll likely find yourself constantly pulling the lower-right corner of the browser window back and forth to appreciate the effects you're about to create—many of your users will never see it. Most visitors will come to a website with their browser at a set width and leave it unchanged for the duration of their visit, especially mobile users, who do not have an option of changing viewport sizes. Many of the techniques you'll explore in this chapter should therefore be considered "nice to have" rather than required.

Later in the chapter, you'll look at how JavaScript can be integrated with CSS3 Animations and Transitions to make them more effective and efficient.

Resizing Elements in Responsive Web Design Without Transitions

Using the principles I discussed above you can "animate" a web page's content on viewport resize without using transitions or keyframe animations at all.

Dynamically Resizing Images and Videos

First, you'll resize images and videos in response to viewport size (see Figure 8-1).

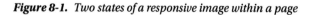

Figure 8-1. *Two states of a responsive image within a page*

By sizing elements relative to their containers, you can smoothly "animate" the size of the elements as the browser window is resized. Technically, this isn't animation at all. At this stage, you're simply sizing an image dynamically by scaling it relative to its container (see Listing 8-1).

Listing 8-1. A Responsive Image

```
html { font-size: 62.5%; }
p { font-size: 1rem; }
.left { max-width: 100%; height: auto; float: left; margin-right: 2rem; margin-bottom: 1rem; }
<section>
<p><img src="pentacon-bike.jpg" alt="Pentacon Bike" class="left">Lorem ipsum dolor sit amet...
</section>
```

As they resize the browser users will have the impression that the image (supplied by filtran, `www.flickr.com/photos/filtran/2978448269/`) is being dynamically resized. The photograph will be displayed at its natural size if the browser is set wide enough, but will scale to fit viewport widths that cannot contain its full dimension.

There are two possible drawbacks to this approach: depending on the initial native size of the image relative to the body text, the image may appear out-of-scale at large or small screen widths. Alternatively, you can set the image as a percentage of the width of its container, so that it scales down through the entire range of the viewport. For example, let's say that you've determined that a decent overall size for the paragraphs is 900 pixels wide, with 90 characters per measure (line of text). Given the presentational rule for the HTML and paragraphs, this means that the width of the section element would equate to 90rem. The natural size of the image is 425 pixels wide. To make the image completely scalable, you translate all of these values to percentages:

```
425 / 900 = 0.4722
```

This means that the image takes up 47.22% of the width of the paragraphs and translates to the CSS you see in Listing 8-2.

Listing 8-2. An Alternate Responsive Image

```
section { max-width: 90rem; }
.left { width: 47.22%; height: auto; float: left; margin-right: 2.5%; margin-bottom: 2%; }
```

This combination of CSS declarations will create the appearance of the page shown in Figure 8-2.

Lorem ipsum dolor sit amet, consectetur adipiscing elit. Suspendisse dictum rhoncus euismod. Suspendisse sed diam eros, sit amet condimentum arcu. In rhoncus velit eu nisl convallis laoreet. Curabitur ut ultrices ipsum. Vestibulum viverra ultrices sapien, nec fermentum risus sagittis nec. Quisque erat libero, tempus porttitor convallis a, ultrices id justo. Nam at accumsan elit. Nunc in nibh velit, a vulputate urna. Class aptent taciti sociosqu ad litora torquent per conubia nostra, per inceptos himenaeos. Aliquam aliquam sollicitudin lobortis. Pellentesque ante nibh, luctus auctor accumsan id, pretium sit amet erat. Donec odio magna, mollis et ultricies ac, congue vel libero. Mauris in pellentesque sapien.

Sed porta nisi ac eros tincidunt ut aliquet nulla luctus. Donec fringilla, nisl nec tincidunt tempus, leo risus facilisis magna, a molestie dui quam vitae orci. Praesent pellentesque, ipsum sed sollicitudin lacinia, lorem mi accumsan nibh, in imperdiet metus metus sit amet tortor. Proin id lectus purus, eget volutpat diam. Donec non felis velit. Nullam fermentum scelerisque laoreet. Aliquam erat volutpat. Nullam sit amet est nisl, in pulvinar felis. Morbi sapien leo, dapibus ac ultrices ac, convallis imperdiet turpis. Praesent euismod luctus sapien in porttitor. Donec ultricies odio vitae est tempus lacinia. Aliquam dapibus feugiat sem eu viverra. Donec erat magna, bibendum quis gravida et, vestibulum in tellus. Quisque lorem dui, lobortis ut vestibulum ac, pretium ut nibh.

Aenean porttitor ipsum eget ipsum laoreet ac egestas metus iaculis. Fusce a justo quis mi hendrerit blandit. Proin dapibus odio viverra leo mattis vitae egestas turpis mattis. Ut eget sodales nulla. Sed et lobortis urna. Suspendisse potenti. Nunc tempor imperdiet erat ut cursus. Ut tristique interdum turpis nec convallis. Etiam diam risus, convallis pretium mollis non, adipiscing interdum nulla.

Lorem ipsum dolor sit amet, consectetur adipiscing elit. Suspendisse dictum rhoncus euismod. Suspendisse sed diam eros, sit amet condimentum arcu. In rhoncus velit eu nisl convallis laoreet. Curabitur ut ultrices ipsum. Vestibulum viverra ultrices sapien, nec fermentum risus sagittis nec. Quisque erat libero, tempus porttitor convallis a, ultrices id justo. Nam at accumsan elit. Nu in nibh velit, a vulputate urna. Class aptent taciti sociosqu ad litora torquent per conubia nostra, per inceptos himenaeos. Aliquam aliquam sollicitudin lobortis. Pellentesque ante nibh, luctus auctor accumsan id, pretium sit amet erat. Donec odio magna, mollis et ultricies ac, congue vel libero. Mauris in pellentesque sapien.

Sed porta nisi ac eros tincidunt ut aliquet nulla luctus. Donec fringilla, nisl nec tincidunt tempus, leo risus facilisis magna, a molestie dui quam vitae orci. Praesent pellentesque, ipsum sec sollicitudin lacinia, lorem mi accumsan nibh, in imperdiet metu: metus sit amet tortor. Proin id lectus purus, eget volutpat diam. Donec non felis velit. Nullam fermentum scelerisque laoreet. Aliquam erat volutpat. Nullam sit amet est nisl, in pulvinar felis. Morbi sapien leo, dapibus ac ultrices ac, convallis imperdiet turpis. Praesent euismod luctus sapien in porttitor. Donec ultric odio vitae est tempus lacinia. Aliquam dapibus feugiat sem eu viverra. Donec erat magna, bibendum quis gravida et, vestibulum in tellus. Quisque lorem dui, lobortis ut vestibulum

Figure 8-2. *An alternate responsive image*

The one remaining problem is the potential for very large or very small images to be created at extreme viewport sizes. You might wish to protect the design by setting minimum and maximum sizes to the image (see Listing 8-3).

Listing 8-3. A Responsive Image with a Minimum and Maximum Size

```
.left { width: 47.22%; height: auto; float: left;
    margin-right: 2.5%; margin-bottom: 2%;
    max-width: 425px; min-width: 150px;
}
```

You can achieve the same effect on <video> elements using the same technique. (Making a video responsive when it is embedded via a service such as YouTube or Vimeo is significantly trickier; I'd recommend Dave Ruppert's FitVids JQuery plugin at http://fitvidsjs.com/ to achieve that).

■ **Tip** It's also possible to resize text dynamically without using keyframes, transitions, or media queries. The vw unit measures the viewport width: 1vw is 1/100th of the width of the browser window. So if the viewport is 400 pixels wide, 1vw would be equivalent to 4px. You can use this unit to scale your text as the browser resizes:

```
h1 { font-size: 4vw; }
```

With this CSS, h1 elements on the web page will resize as the browser expands and contracts. You can also use vh and vw on other elements as well.

Responsive Background Images

You can easily resize background images dynamically in response to viewport changes by using the background-size property (here using an image by Vinoth Chandar at www.flickr.com/photos/vinothchandar/6168933212/) as in Listing 8-4.

Listing 8-4. A Responsive Background Image

```
html, body { min-height: 100%; font-size: 62.5%; }
body { background-image: url(fog.jpg); background-size: cover; }
```

Combined with some body text, this gives the effect shown in Figure 8-3.

Figure 8-3. *A responsive background image*

For other ways to "transition" background images, see Chapter 3.

Resizing Elements in Responsive Web Design with Transitions

It's entirely possible to transition elements between @media query breakpoints. From a design perspective, the major issue to be aware of is the element's potential "jump" between states on viewport resize, which may be surprising to the user.

Let's create a design that has a large h1 element in the middle of the page, above a photograph (Listing 8-5).

Listing 8-5. HTML for a Responsive Background Image and Transitioned Text

```
body { background-image: url(fog.jpg); background-size: cover;
    background-repeat: no-repeat; color: #fff; font-family: Avenir, Arial, sans-serif;
}
h1 { font-family: 'Calluna Sans', Arial, sans-serif; text-align: center;
    font-size: 10rem; margin: 8rem auto;
}
```

As the viewport narrows, the heading text will naturally break at spaces, as shown in Figure 8-4.

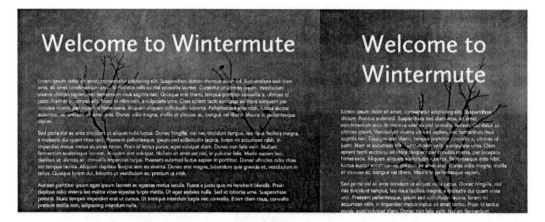

Figure 8-4. *A nonresponsive heading element breaking on spaces under a narrow viewport*

If instead we wanted to keep the heading on a single line, we could reduce the size of the text at the breakpoints and transition between them as shown in Listing 8-6.

Listing 8-6. HTML for a Responsive Background Image and Transitioned Text

```
h1 { font-family: 'Calluna Sans', Arial, sans-serif;
    text-align: center; font-size: 10rem; margin: 8rem auto; transition: 1s font-size linear;
}
@media screen and (max-width: 1100px) {
      h1 { font-size: 8rem; }
}
@media screen and (max-width: 900px) {
      h1 { font-size: 7rem; }
}
@media screen and (max-width: 800px) {
      h1 { font-size: 6rem; }
}
```

The code shown in Listing 8-6 gives you the result shown in Figure 8-5.

Figure 8-5. *A responsive heading element*

Indicating Viewport Size with CSS3 Media Queries and Transitions

Using media queries, you can trigger an element to "morph" in appearance as the browser is narrowed—for example, to show different viewing modes in a responsive page, so that users understand that they are not looking at a simple interpretation of a desktop site on a mobile platform, but at a page that is customizing itself to the size of the browser window (see Figure 8-6).

Figure 8-6. *A responsive transitioned symbol in three different states, representing three different viewport sizes*

First of all, you will set up a series of breakpoints:

- 120em wide and above will be considered "widescreen".

- At 80em wide you can assume the user is viewing the site with a tablet.

- At 40em and below you should assume the user is using a smartphone.

Next you create the elements that will be used to show these various states from pure CSS. There will be a total of three elements: a containing div with an absolute position that will keep all of the elements in the top-right corner of the screen; a span representing the display, and another span representing the base or button, as shown in Listing 8-7.

Listing 8-7. HTML Code for a Transitioned Display Mode in a Responsive Page

```
<div id="viewingmode">
        <span id="display"></span>
        <span id="buttonbase"></span>
</div>
```

Next, you'll create the base CSS for the elements in Listing 8-8. This will include the transition settings.

Listing 8-8. CSS Code to Create Viewing Mode Symbols in a Responsive Design

```
* { box-sizing: border-box; }
body { font-family: Avenir, sans-serif; margin: 100px 0; }
#viewingmode {
    width: 150px; height: 150px; background: rgba(0,0,0,0.2);
    position: absolute; top: 0; right: 0; text-align: center;
}

/* screen, in default widescreen presentation */
```

```
#display {
    width: 80%; height: 50%; border: 12px solid #585858;
    border-radius: 5px; margin-top: 20px; background-color: #eee;
}

/* base, in default monitor stand - keyboard configuration */

#buttonbase {
    width: 90px; border: 12px solid #585858; border-radius: 5px;
    position: absolute; top: 100px; left: 30px; transform-origin: 25px 5px;
}
#display, #buttonbase { display: inline-block; transition: .5s all linear; }
```

Finally, you'll create the media queries to change the appearance of the #display and #buttonbase elements (Listing 8-6). Note that these alterations cascade: smaller screen sizes will inherit the changes made in media queries for larger screens.

Listing 8-6. CSS Code to Create Viewing Mode Symbols in a Responsive Design

```
@media screen and (max-width: 80em) {
    #display { width: 50%; height: 60%; border: 10px solid #585858; }
    #buttonbase { width: 8px; height: 8px; border: none;
        border-radius: 50%; background: #fff; top: 101px; left: 70px; }
}
@media screen and (max-width: 40em) {
    #display { border-width: 23px 5px; width: 45%; height: 73%; }
    #buttonbase { top: 110px;    }
}
```

As noted, most users—especially mobile users—will not see these animations because mobile devices have fixed screen widths and nothing to adjust to. An alternative approach might be to show whether the screen is being held in portrait or landscape mode, as shown in Listing 8-7.

Listing 8-7. Media Queries to Show Landscape and Portrait Mode on a Device

```
@media screen and (orientation: landscape) and (max-width: 80em) {
    #display { transform: rotate(90deg);    }
    }
```

This creates the changing displays you see illustrated in Figure 8-6, with each device "morphing" into the next as the viewport is resized based on the orientation of the device. The same principles can be applied to animate many different aspects of web pages with responsive design.

Optimizing CSS Transitions and Animations for Mobile Devices

It is inevitable that the processors in mobile devices will grow faster and more powerful over time, but they will always lag behind the abilities of full desktop models. It is also inevitable that developers will tend to code for the platform in front of their noses, rather than what their audience may be using (as we saw during the browser wars and in vendor prefix biases). Developers write code for the screen in front of them, the result of which may not always scale down to the more restricted abilities of mobile devices.

There are several possible ways to improve CSS effects that run slow on mobile devices:

- *Try to funnel transitions and optimizations through the GPU of the device*: Due to their more complex and demanding nature, many browsers will attempt to smooth 3D transforms, transitions, and animations (covered in Chapter 9) by pipelining them through the specialized Graphic Processing Unit of the device on which the CSS animation is running. You can hitch a ride on this optimized stream by starting a CSS declaration block with an "empty" 3D manipulation that will not visually alter the element, but will allow access to the GPU to the 2D transforms that follow in the same declaration:

```
transform: translate3d(0,0,0);
```

■ **Note**   Remy Sharp has a very effective video showing the advantage of funneling transitions and optimizations through a device's GPU on YouTube at `www.youtube.com/watch?v=IKl78ZgJzm4`.

- *Limit or substitute animations with media queries*: You can set up more limited versions of animations for mobile devices by creating different versions under an @media query.

- *Ensure that pages containing animated elements will scale down completely to mobile screen sizes*: Animations that are cut off at the edges will obviously not look good or perform effectively on a mobile device.

Integrating CSS3 Media Queries with SVG

You can also use media queries (among other CSS3 features) to target elements in SVG.

Just like Adobe PhotoShop and other graphics applications, SVG includes the concept of multiple layers. This means you can merge multiple drawings into one SVG file and switch the visibility of each using CSS.

Let's return to the idea of placing icons in the top-right corner of the browser window, but make them SVG instead; in this case, a series of grouped SVG drawings of different body types, including the *mesomorph* and *ectomorph* types. For the sake of space, code for only the first body type is shown in the simplified Listing 8-8.

Listing 8-8. SVG File of Multiple Drawing Layers

```
<svg version="1.1" xmlns="http://www.w3.org/2000/svg" width="142px" height="340px"
viewBox="0 0 142 340">
<style>
    g { visibility: hidden;  }
    g:target  { visibility: visible;  }
</style>
    <g id="ectomorph">
            <path d="M11.356,682.57c5.297,6.354,10.253,10.084,17.781,14.844
            C18.907,694.043,15.905,690.475,11.356,682.57z"/>
. . . .
    </g>
<g id="mesomorph">
    <path d="M9.981,679.538c0,0-8.719,7.188-8.719,17.125 ..." />
. . . .
</g>
```

Each of the grouped SVG drawings is layered on top of one another, as shown in Figure 8-7. The layers are then hidden with CSS. The next line in the embedded stylesheet turns on the visibility of a group if a URL targets it. You can use CSS to place the SVG file as a background image in a div, as shown in Listing 8-9.

Figure 8-7. *Different named layers of an SVG vector drawing superimposed on each other*

Listing 8-9. SVG File of Multiple Drawing Layers

```
div#shapes { background-image: url('bodyshapes.svg#mesomorph');
position: absolute; top: 0; right: 0; width: 145px; height: 355px;  }
```

Using the same targeting technique, you can swap the visibility of the layers in the SVG file used in the background image of the div (Listing 8-10).

Listing 8-10. SVG File of Multiple Drawing Layers

```
@media screen and (max-width: 1000px) {
    div#shapes { background-image: url('bodyshapes.svg#ectomorph); }
}
```

Finally, it should be noted that SVG elements can be animated in and of themselves with the `<animate />` element, The visibility of each layer can be animated with transitions if the SVG was inserted directly on the page, rather than having been used as a background image.

Triggering CSS3 Transitions with JavaScript

JavaScript can be used to trigger transitions and animations in CSS3. For example, you could have elements fade in when users reaches the bottom of a page to increase their interest in related content (see Figure 8-8). CSS cannot detect the state of the scrollbar—you need to use JavaScript to do that and then animate the elements that appear using CSS3.

Sed placerat, massa ut ultrices fringilla, magna diam ornare est, vel lobortis libero urna nec eros. Maecenas lobortis purus ac dui facilisis faucibus egestas nunc consectetur. Fusce ipsum dolor, laoreet id laoreet ac, varius vitae magna. Aliquam erat volutpat. Morbi ut eros ut nunc pulvinar lacinia eu at ligula. Praesent sit amet nibh non ligula molestie eleifend at eu nisl. Mauris in velit sit amet risus tempus rutrum nec ac lectus. Integer sapien magna, ultrices ut eleifend ut, adipiscing molestie nisl. Nulla auctor turpis ut tortor dignissim vel mattis ipsum sagittis. Praesent aliquam erat vitae tortor varius ac eleifend turpis tristique.

 ◄ Cicero and Claudius

Caligula and Ceasar  ►

Figure 8-8. Footer elements animated with CSS transitions triggered by JQuery

> ■ **Note** There is an argument to be made that if you're initiating an animation with JavaScript, you might as well continue to create the animation in that same language. However, as discussed in Chapter 1, CSS3 transitions will be smoother and more efficient, and will achieve a higher frame rate than what you can achieve in JavaScript. There is a reason libraries such as JQuery Transit (`http://ricostacruz.com/jquery.transit/`) and Move. js (`http://visionmedia.github.com/move.js`) are increasingly being used to hook JavaScript into CSS3 Transition and Animation methods. This separation of functions reflects a separation between content, presentation, and behavior: in this example, JavaScript is used to detect DOM events, and CSS is used to present *changes in appearance* to that content.

First, let's assume that you have more than enough content to fill the viewport: I'll show a heading and a fragment of *Lorem ipsum* filler text in Listing 8-11 to indicate the start of the body text. At the very bottom of the page you'll have two links inside a `footer` element. The first link will lead the user to content that is logically "previous" to the page they are currently on; the second link, to the right, will direct them to the "next" page after the current one. I've used Unicode black left- and right-pointing triangle shapes inside the links to save space: you should use the appropriate HTML entities (◀ and ▶ respectively) instead.

Listing 8-11. HTML Code for an Extra-Long Page with Content in a Footer Engaged with JavaScript and CSS3 Transitions

```
...
    <script src="//ajax.googleapis.com/ajax/libs/jquery/1.8/jquery.min.js"></script>
</head>
<body>
<article>
    <header><h1>A History of the Roman Empire</h1></header>
    <p>Lorem ipsum dolor sit amet, consectetur adipiscing elit...
```

```
<footer id="articlefooter">
    <a href=# id=prevpage>◀<img src=cicero.png alt=Cicero>Cicero and Claudius</a>
    <a href=# id=nextpage>Caligula and Ceasar <img src=caesar.png alt=Caeasar>▶</a>
</footer>
</article>
</body>
```

The footer should be pushed below the bottom edge of the viewport window by the content in the article. You're going to style the page, indenting the links in the footer slightly and making them invisible by lowering their opacity (Listing 8-12).

Listing 8-12. Base CSS Code for a Page with Footer Navigation

```
body { font-family: Avenir, sans-serif; margin: 100px 0; }
article { width: 768px; margin: 0 auto; }
footer#articlefooter { padding: 0 25px; }
footer#articlefooter a {
    text-decoration: none; color: #000; opacity: 0;  position: relative;
}
footer#articlefooter a img { width: 77px; height: 77ps; vertical-align: middle; }
a#prevpage { padding-left: 70px; float: left; transition: 1s 1s opacity linear, 1s 1s translateX ↵
linear; }
a#nextpage { padding-right: 70px; float: right; transition: 1s .5s opacity linear, 1s 1s ↵
translateX linear; }
```

You've associated the CSS3 transition code with the links: if they are fired at the same time, .linkmoveright, associated with the #nextarticle element, will move first. After a short delay, it will be followed by the .linkmoveleft class, associated with #prevarticle.

Note that you have made the transition more efficient by declaring the properties you are changing: because they are multiple properties, you use a repetition separated by a comma.

Rather than associate the changes to the elements that will be initiated by your transitions with a :hover or :focus pseudo-selector, you're going to define them as a new class (see Listing 8-13).

Listing 8-13. Transforms for Footer Navigational Elements

```
.linkmoveleft { transform: translateX(-70px); opacity: 1; }
.linkmoveright  { transform: translateX(70px);  opacity: 1; }
```

Finally, you're going to add a script at the very bottom of the page that will look at a few variables and judge when to add these classes to the elements.

As used in Listing 8-14, the articleheight variable determines the overall height of the body, including all of its content. scrollTop measures how many pixels of the page are *above* the top edge of the browser window: this will be 0 when the page loads, with the value increasing as the user scrolls down. By dividing articleheight by 2 and comparing the result to scrollTop, you can determine when the user has scrolled through half the page and then apply the classes (Listing 8-14).

Listing 8-14. JQuery Code to Place Classes on Navigational Footer Elements

```
<script>
$(function() {
    var articleheight = $("body").height();
    $(window).scroll(function() {
```

```
        if ($(this).scrollTop() > (articleheight / 2)) {
            $("#prevpage").toggleClass("linkmoveleft");
            $("#nextpage").toggleClass("linkmoveright");

    });
});
</script>
```

CSS3 transitions will fire in response to *any* appropriate change in the state of the elements they are associated with , whether those changes are imposed by CSS, JavaScript, or anything else. In this case, the placing of new classes that contain changes to the elements' opacity and position with JQuery is enough to set off the transitions.

While this works, looking at the results critically reveals that the approach has several possible drawbacks:

- Particularly long articles may feature body text that is more than twice the height of the browser window. The comparison in the script in Listing 8-14 means that for such articles the transitions may fire before the user has reached the bottom of the page (i.e., after reading more than half the article they still may not see the footer).

- The `toggleClass` function means that JQuery will try to undo the application of the classes when the user scrolls upward and fire them again when the user returns to the bottom of the page. Such repeated transitions could prove annoying.

- Finally, we are assuming that the footer will always be congruent with the bottom of the page. This is not necessarily true: there may be comments beneath the footer, which would extend the overall height of the article significantly, causing the JavaScript to apply the classes early.

■ **Note**   Under the HTML5 specification, article elements nested inside another article are assumed to contain commentary on the parent.

As an alternative approach, apply the transitions just once when the footer is clearly on the page (Listing 8-15).

Listing 8-15. Improved JQuery Code to Place Classes on Navigational Footer Elements

```
$(function() {
    var footerBottom = $("#articlefooter").offset().top + $("#articlefooter").height();
        $(window).scroll(function() {
            if ($(this).scrollTop() > (footerBottom - $(window).height())) {
                $("#prevpage").addClass("linkmoveleft");
                $("#nextpage").addClass("linkmoveright");
            }
        });
});
```

If you wanted to support Internet Explorer 6 through 8, you could use Modernizr (http://modernizr.com/) to detect browser support of CSS transitions. If the browser lacked support, JQuery could fall back on animating the elements itself (see Listing 8-16).

Listing 8-16. Improved JQuery Code to Place Classes on Navigational Footer Elements

```
<script src=//ajax.googleapis.com/ajax/libs/jquery/1.8/jquery.min.js></script>
<script src=scripts/modernizr.js></script>
</head>
<body>
<article>

. . .

</article>
<script>
$(function() {
    var footerBottom = $("#articlefooter").offset().top + $("#articlefooter").height();
    $(window).scroll(function() {
        if ($(this).scrollTop() > (footerBottom - $(window).height())) {
            if (Modernizr.csstransitions) {
                    $("#prevpage").addClass("linkmoveleft");
                    $("#nextpage").addClass("linkmoveright");
                        } else {
                    $("#prevpage").animate({ opacity: 1, left: '-=70'}, 1000, function() {
});
                    $("#nextpage").animate({ opacity: 1, left: '+=70'}, 1000, function() {
});
                        }
                }
    });
});
</script>
```

If you wanted to create a more complex effect, you could write keyframe animations and either apply them as classes, as in Listing 8-16, or inject the call to the animations directly using JQuery. For a final example, you will use the latter approach, calling keyframe animations that duplicate the effect you just created with transitions (Listing 8-17).

Listing 8-17. JQuery Code Used to Apply CSS3 Animations

```
@keyframes leftmove {
        100% { transform: translateX(-70px);  opacity: 1; }
}

@keyframes rightmove {
        100% { transform: translateX(70px);  opacity: 1; }
}

<script>
$(function() {
    var footerBottom = $("#articlefooter").offset().top + $("#articlefooter").height();
    $(window).scroll(function() {
        if ($(this).scrollTop() > (footerBottom - $(window).height())) {
```

```
            $("#prevpage").css('animation', 'leftmove 1s 2s forwards');
            $("#nextpage").css('animation', 'rightmove 1s 1s forwards');
    });
});
</script>
```

■ **Note** The technique shown in Listing 8-17 can be used to avoid the semantically questionable approach to interactivity demonstrated in Chapter 4 by using `form` label and `checkbox` buttons. Rather than jumping through markup hoops to achieve the results you want in CSS, you can simply employ JavaScript to detect DOM events on any element and initiate CSS3 transformations, transitions, and animations on others, as shown in Listing 8-18.

Listing 8-18. JQuery Code Used to Apply a CSS3 Animation on Click

```
$(function() {
    $("#at").click(function() { $(".box").toggleClass("wobble"); });
});
```

Customizing CSS3 Transitions with JavaScript

In Chapter 6 you looked at animating multiple SVG elements with CSS3. When doing so you encountered a major issue: to animate elements you had to create them as individual elements on the page, making it difficult to create the appearance of randomness (see Figure 8-9).

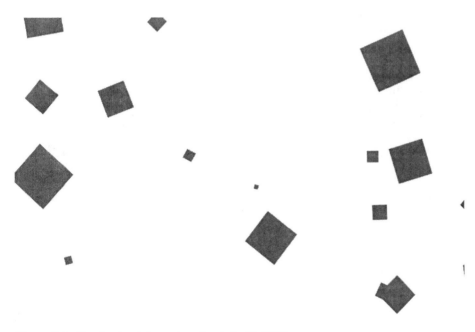

Figure 8-9. *Randomized elements animated with CSS3*

In an effort to reduce the amount of hand-coding you have to do in any page, you will use JavaScript to solve both of these issues. To keep things simple, you use red `div` elements as the animated objects. At the bottom of a page you'll add the script shown in Listing 8-19.

Listing 8-19. JavaScript Code to Create Random Scattered Elements

```
<script>
var html = [];
for (i = 0; i < 30; i++) {
    var randomX = Math.random() * (100 - 1) + 1;
    var randomY = Math.random() * (1200 - 1) + 1;
    var randomZ = Math.random() * (100 - 1) + 1;
html.push('<div style="left:'+randomX+'%;top:'+randomY+'px;width:'+randomZ+'px;height: ↵
'+randomZ+'>
</div>');
}
    $("body").append( html.join('') );
</script>
```

You use a JavaScript loop to create as many copies of the `div` element as you wish. For each element, you'll use three variables to determine its horizontal position, offset from the top edge of the viewport, together with the horizontal and vertical size.

However many elements you have will all follow the same keyframe animation rules shown in Listing 8-20.

Listing 8-20. JavaScript Code to Create Random Scattered Elements

```
html { height: 100%; }
body { min-height: 100%; margin: 0; }
@keyframes snowflake {
        100% { transform: translateY(1800px) rotate(1200deg);  }
}
div { background: red; position: absolute; animation: snowflake 40s linear infinite;  }
```

Although this works, there are several issues: all of the shapes fall at the same rate, and turn synchronously. An element that is small appears to be further away, and should fall more slowly, while all elements should start at a randomized rotation. In order to achieve this, you'll create several classes that will call the keyframe animation with different timings and apply the classes with JavaScript, based on the element's size (Listing 8-21).

Listing 8-21. CSS and JavaScript Code to Create Randomized Scattered Elements

```
<style>
@keyframes snowflake {
    100% { transform: translateY(1800px) rotate(1200deg);  }
}
div { background: red; position: absolute;
animation-name: snowflake;
animation-iteration-count: infinite;
animation-timing-function: linear;
}
.small { animation-duration: 40s; }
.medium { animation-duration: 20s; }
.large { animation-duration: 10s; }
</style>
```

```
<body>
...
</body>

<script>
var html = [];
for (i = 0; i < 30; i++) {
    var randomX = Math.random() * (100 - 1) + 1;
    var randomY = Math.random() * (1200 - 1) + 1;
    var randomZ = Math.random() * (100 - 1) + 1;
    var randomR = Math.random() * (360 - 1) + 1;
    var sizes = ['small','medium','large'];
    var dim = sizes[Math.round(randomX/50)];
    html.push('<div style="left:'+randomX+'%;top:- ↵
'+randomY+'px;width:'+randomZ+'px;height:'+randomZ+'px;transform:translateY(0px) ↵
rotate('+randomR+'deg)" class='+dim+'></div>');
}
$("body").append( html.join('') );
</script>
```

This JavaScript code is basic and could be taken much further, but the important aspect to be aware of is that you are making use of the core strengths of each of these technologies: you use CSS to provide rules for appearance and JavaScript to make rapid changes to the DOM.

Summary

This chapter provided an introduction to the integration of CSS3 Animations, Transforms, and Transitions with responsive web design, JavaScript, and SVG. You can create the impression of "animated" elements in response to viewport resizing by scaling content using percentage and vw units, and using @media queries to animate elements at breakpoints.

You can also use JavaScript to provide trigger points for animations that CSS itself cannot detect, and use the scripting language to make multiple randomized "clones" of elements for animation sequences. The integration of these technologies can be taken much further: a good example is Sebastian Markbåge's solution to the technical difficulty of having an element follow a complex path at a constant rate of motion by using SVG path data to generate keyframe animation declarations (http://csspathanimation.calyptus.eu/).

In this book so far, you've been using CSS3 to move elements across the flat plane surface of the page. In the next chapter, you will manipulate HTML elements in 3D space.

■ ■ ■

CHAPTER 9

CSS3 3D Transforms, Transitions, and Animations

So far you've manipulated images, UI elements, and other web content in the flat planar space of the viewport. But using the scale transform doesn't necessarily imply that an element is further away from the viewer, only that it is larger or smaller; using standard CSS fails to impart a true sense of perspective or depth.

The 3D properties of the CSS Transforms module change all that. 3D Transforms allow you to manipulate content in a projected 3D space. Those 3D-projected elements can then be animated using the transition or keyframe syntax you've explored in previous chapters.

3D Transforms are one aspect of CSS3 that tend *not* to degrade well in the browser: if the 3D transform declarations are not understood by the client, elements will usually appear stacked on top of each other. You should carefully consider this before rendering elements in older browsers

Although they can be used as such, CSS 3D Tranforms are not intended to make entire web sites a "3D environment" in which the browser window spins between one page and another. Rather, the new properties are typically used much as the rest of CSS is used: to make presentational choices for some elements on a web page. Creating and interacting with entire "worlds" of 3D content is best left to the context of the canvas element, through technologies such as WebGL.

Due to their heavier computational demands, 3D transforms are pipelined directly to the client's GPU, providing a high frame rate during animation.

Perspective

The key to transforming HTML elements in 3D space is perspective, which can be specified as a CSS property:

```
#ngc-1763 { perspective: 600px; }
```

It can also be specified as a value in transform:

```
#ngc-1763 { transform: perspective(600px); }
```

Both methods are exactly equivalent and produce the same result. Naturally, both methods will require vendor prefixes to gain support in older browsers.

Note that you will not see any difference after applying perspective alone. Setting perspective is a necessary precursor to 3D manipulation, but does not change an element's appearance in and of itself.

perspective can take any positive CSS length value and defines the *distance from the viewpoint to the 3D element*. This may be the most difficult aspect of 3D transforms to understand, which is why this property deserves greater consideration than some others. The perspective property is illustrated in Figure 9-1.

(The image shown here is from Per Ola Wiberg, at `www.flickr.com/photos/powi`, used by permission, as are all the photographs used in this chapter).

Figure 9-1. *Changes to perspective in 3D transforms creates different visual results*

In the image on the left, the viewpoint is relatively close to the affected elements; the perspective gained by setting to 200px is similar to viewing the scene through a camera's macro lens. 3D changes are likely to appear dramatic and distorted. In the image on the right, the viewpoint (set to 2000px) is distant from the affected elements, rendering the content relatively "flat", as if viewed through a telephoto lens. Visual transforms in 3D space are more likely to be subtle and understated.

While individual elements may have separate `perspective` properties applied to them, doing so implies that each element has its own visual origin, and will be displayed unrelated to other elements in 3D space. Transformation of the elements means that each will show a different vanishing point while potentially taxing the browser more as it calculates the independent orientations of each element. Unless you are deliberately aiming for an *Inception*-like effect, it is recommended that you apply `perspective` just once to a *parent* element that contains the content you wish to manipulate in 3D space. A containing `div` or possibly the body element itself can both work well. With the `perspective` declaration in place on the right element, 3D transforms of its child elements will create a consistent visual appearance, as shown in the right-side image of Figure 9-2.

Figure 9-2. *Changes to perspective in 3D transforms creates different visual results*

Just as 2D transforms have a `transform-origin`, 3D transforms have a `perspective-origin` that defaults to the center of the element. While it is not wrong to place the `perspective-origin` elsewhere (using any CSS length or appropriate keyword, horizontal followed by vertical location relative to the element), you should be aware that using high values when doing so can produce extreme visual distortion, such as isometric effects. An individual element with its own `perspective` has its `perspective-origin` "buried" inside itself, muting the effect of most 3D manipulations. Placing the `perspective`—and by association, the `perspective-origin`—in the parent element will usually provide better visual results.

Let's take a look at these effects visually. Both screenshots in Figure 9-2 share the same basic code shown in Listing 9-1.

Listing 9-1. HTML and CSS Shared for a Simple 3D-Manipulated Image Gallery

```
<style>
    html { height: 100%;  }
    body { min-height: 100%; background: #333;  margin: 60px; }
    img {  width: 300px; height: 300px; margin: 30px; }
</style>

<body>
    <img src=waterlily.jpg alt="Gul Näckros Waterlily">
    <img src=red-tulip.jpg alt="Red Tulip">
    <img src=dahlia.jpg alt=Dahlia>
    <img src=tulips.jpg alt=Tulips>
    <img src=tarda-tulip.jpg alt="Tarda Tulip">
    <img src=applebloom.jpg alt="Sweet applebloom">
    <img src=yellow-tulip.jpg alt="Yellow tulip">
    <img src=orchid.jpg alt=Orchid>
    <img src=poppy.jpg alt="Blue Himalyan poppy">
</body>
```

In Figure 9-2, the left-hand screenshot has `perspective` and `perspective-origin` applied to the individual images, while the right-hand screenshot shows the same properties applied to the body. Both examples have the same rotation applied to the images.

In the image on the left, images are rotated *internally* unto themselves, showing no change in perspective. On the left, images are rotated *relative to* the body perspective, transformed from a consistent vanishing point.

It's interesting to note that in the second example, the 3D effect is responsive: because the `perspective-origin` is on the right side of the body, adjusting the browser window changes the position of the origin and thus alters the vanishing point for all 3D elements. Widening and narrowing the browser will cause the image elements to rotate as they remain in alignment with the changing perspective origin.

When placing `perspective-origin` be extra-aware of the default behaviors in CSS for elements: container elements with floated child elements having no height, for example, or the body being the height of its content by default. These aspects can have significant influences when placing the origin and manipulating content in an implied 3D space.

To demonstrate this, take the HTML code in Listing 9-1, but substitute the CSS in Listing 9-2.

Listing 9-2. CSS Showing Unanticipated Limitations on 3D CSS Perspective

```
body { perspective: 1200px; perspective-origin: center center; margin: 2rem; }
img { width: 500px; height: 375px; float: left; margin-right: 2rem; margin-bottom: 2rem;  }
img {  transform: rotateY(45deg); }
```

The CSS code sets the `perspective-origin` for the body element to its default value of `center` for both the X and Y axes, but as you can see from Figure 9-3, the effect on the images shows that the origin is not at the center of the document, but at the top.

Figure 9-3. *Incorrect orientation of images due to misaligned perspective origin*

To get the perspective on the images correct, you must make the body element at least as high as the content it contains. In this case, you'll use the standard min-height: 100% on the html and height: 100% on the body approach , which you can see in Listing 9-3. Once the CSS3 value is supported in browsers, you will be able to use min-height: contain-floats on the body element alone.

Listing 9-3. CSS 3D Perspective Corrected for Body Height

```
html { height: 100%; }
body { perspective: 1200px; perspective-origin: center center; margin: 2rem;
margin-top: 8rem; min-height: 100%; }
img { width: 500px; height: 375px; float: left; margin-right: 2rem; margin-bottom: 2rem;  }
img { transform: rotateY(45deg); }
```

The change to the CSS provides the correct transforms to the images, as you can see in Figure 9-4.

Figure 9-4. Correct orientation of images with corrected body height

As you can see, proper placement of both perspective and perspective-origin, both in the code and the Cartesian space of your web page, can make a significant difference to how your content is displayed.

Rotation

Now that you've done a little rotation in 3D, you should take a moment to explore it completely. 2D Transforms has only one rotation; not surprisingly, 3D has three. What can be confusing is the orientation and effect of those three axes, shown in Figure 9-5.

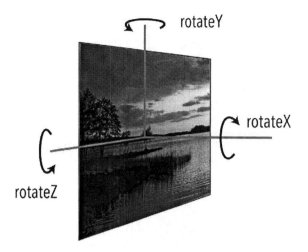

Figure 9-5. *Options for rotation in 3D space*

As you can see, `rotateX` is effectively the same as 2D CSS rotation, and moves *around* the axis like a windmill. `rotateY` swings the element from side-to-side like a door, and `rotateZ` moves around a horizontal axis, like a cat door. Naturally, the visual effect of these transformations will differ as the `perspective-origin` is altered.

If the element is rotated around more than one axis at a time, it's usually more effective to use the `rotate3d` shortcut:

```
img   { transform: rotate3d( 0, 1, 0, 45deg); }
```

You can think of `rotate3d` as a matrix multiplier for each of the axes (x, y, z): if any of the first three slots has any kind of numerical value, the element will be rotated by the last value around the appropriate axes. For example, the above declaration will rotate an image by 45 degrees around the y axis. You can combine multiple rotations by turning on bits for multiple axes:

```
img   { transform: rotate3d( 1, 1, 0, .15turn); }
```

Translate

3D transformed elements can also be moved along the X, Y, and Z axes. Note that doing so will move the element toward or further away from its vanishing point if the element is rotated around the X or Y axes or moved along the Z axis. For example, the code in Listing 9-4 can create the visual effect of an opening crawl for a movie with the credits disappearing into infinite space.

Listing 9-4. Code, Content, and CSS for an Opening Credit Crawl

```
<style>
body { background: #000; perspective: 700px; }
div#crawl { width: 80%; text-align: center; color: #fff;
font-family: 'Franklin Gothic Medium', sans-serif;
font-size: 4rem; margin: 0 auto;
```

```
transform: rotateX(30deg) translateY(-200px); }
</style>
<body>
<div id="crawl">
<h1>Blue Harvest</h1>
<p>The waves of grain moved like the surface of the ocean under the light of the moon, stirred
faintly by a susurrus of wind from the east. Caleb hoisted the worn wooden shaft of a scythe
over his shoulder and peered out into the darkness, dirt-grimed thumbnail scratching under the
brim of his straw hat, just above the sun-seared terminator of skin.</p>
</div>
```

Naturally, this could also easily be animated (Listing 9-5).

Listing 9-5. CSS for an Animated Opening Credit Crawl

```
@keyframes crawl {
    100% { transform: rotateX(40deg) translateY(-2000px);  }
}
div#crawl { transform: rotateX(40deg) translateY(1000px); animation: crawl 30s linear; }
```

This creates the result you see in Figure 9-6.

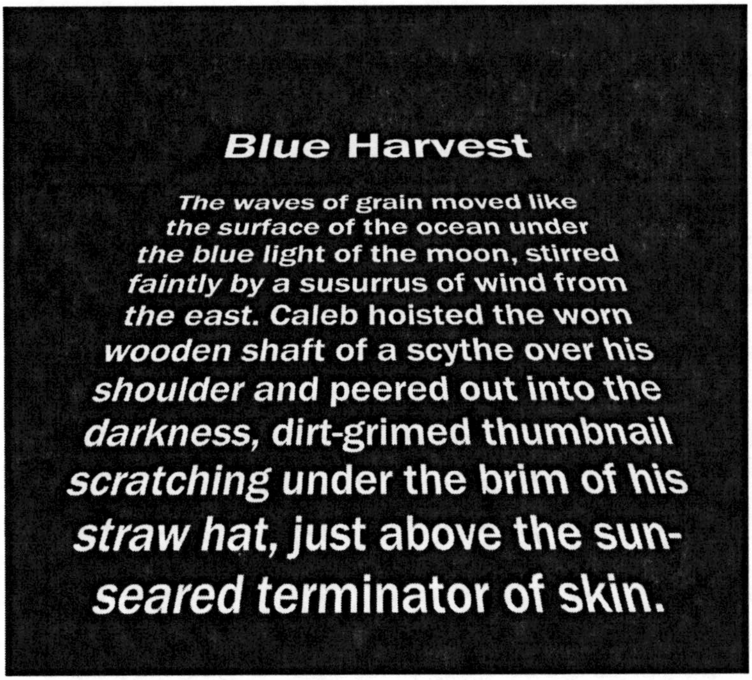

Figure 9-6. *Still from an animated credit crawl created with CSS3*

You can also employ translate3d in the same way the rotate3d property was used previously.

141

■ **Note** Visually there is little difference between `translateZ` and `scaleZ`: they both accomplish the same result, assuming no other tranforms are applied. Otherwise, `scale` works in the same way as the other properties, including `scale3d`.

Card Caption Flip

You can use a combination of these 3D transforms to create several veriations of image captions on the "reverse" side of gallery images, revealed with mouse hover (Figure 9-7).

Figure 9-7. *3D Flipped image caption gallery*

The first example you'll create will use transitions with images in a standard list. All images are exactly the same size, with captions coded as span elements after each one, as shown in Listing 9-6.

Listing 9-6. Code for a Simple 3D Gallery

```
<ul id=gallery>
    <li><img src=tulips.jpg alt="Tulips">
    <span>Tulips</span>
    <li><img src=hepatica-nobilis.jpg alt=Nepatica-nobilis>
    <span style=padding-left:4rem>Nepatica nobilis</span>
    <li><img src=ekebyhosparken.jpg alt=Ekebyhosparken>
    <span style=padding-left:4rem>Ekebyhosparken</span>
</ul>
```

In this example, each image will flip horizontally on mouseover to show its back or reverse face, as if you were looking through a transparency of the image from the other side. After a pause, the span content will fade in over the top of this reversed image (the inline padding is used simply to move the text around inside the span space). Moving the mouse off the image will reverse this sequence. (See Listing 9-7.)

Listing 9-7. CSS for a Simple 3D Gallery

```
body { background: #fff; font-family: Avenir, Arial, sans-serif;
    font-size: 1.5rem; text-shadow: 3px 3px 2px rgba(0,0,0,0.6); }
ul#gallery { margin-top: 400px; perspective: 1000px;  }
ul#gallery li { display: inline-block; margin: 20px;  }
ul#gallery li img { width: 320px; height: 244px;
    box-shadow: 0px 0px 16px rgba(0,0,0,0.3);
    transition: 1s all linear;
}
```

```
ul#gallery li:hover img { transform: rotateY(180deg); }
ul#gallery li span { position: absolute; width: 320px; height: 244px;
    margin-left: -320px; color: #fff; opacity: 0; background: rgba(0,0,0,0.8); display:
inline-block;
    box-sizing: border-box; padding-top: 6rem; padding-left: 8rem;  }
ul#gallery li:hover span { opacity: 1; transition: 1s 1s opacity linear; }
```

The span element uses the `transition-duration` value to come in immediately after the spin has completed. Each spin is around the image's own center; if you wanted to introduce a little more variability, you could change the `transition-origin` for each element.

As an experiment, leave the span elements visible and untransitioned in your CSS; you'll see that the spinning images rotate *through* the caption text, an effect that you'll have the opportunity to use later. Rather like `z-index`, untransformed content is assumed to exist at a "base layer" of presentation that 3D-projected content can slice through, depending on its position and perspective.

It's also worthwhile to note that the image's `box-shadow` is *not* shown as being thrown on the white page of your body content; rather, the shadow rotates as part of the image, surrounding it. While it is possible in theory to manipulate a separate "shadow" div to provide the impression that it is projected, this takes considerable extra effort.

As a whole, the gallery works well, but visitors seeing the "other side" of the image may be confused. (See Figure 9-8.) Providing the impression that your images are actual cards with a plain reverse side that holds a caption, with all of these elements moving together, requires a little more work.

Nepatica nobilis

Figure 9-8. *3D flipped image caption gallery with solid reverse side*

First, you'll change the markup to provide a page variation with more semantic value, shown in Listing 9-8.

Listing 9-8. Code for a More Complex 3D Gallery

```
<figure>
    <figcaption>Tulips</figcaption>
    <img src=tulips.jpg alt=Tulips>
</figure>
<figure>
    <figcaption>Nepatica nobilis</figcaption>
    <img src=hepatica-nobilis.jpg alt="Nepatica nobilis">
</figure>
<figure>
        <figcaption>Ekebyhosparken</figcaption>
    <img src=ekebyhosparken.jpg alt=Ekebyhosparken>
</figure>
```

Note the source order: each image caption comes *before* the image it references. This is perfectly valid in HTML5, and will be useful for your CSS animation. You could place the captions after the images, but that would require changing the z-index value of the captions. The CSS code starts out in a manner similar to the last example (see Listing 9-9).

Listing 9-9. Basic CSS Code for a More Complex 3D Gallery

```
body { background: hsl(100,0%,100%); font-family: Avenir, sans-serif; font-size: 1.5rem;
    margin-top: 400px; perspective: 1000px;      }
figure { margin: 20px; transition: 1s all linear;
    box-shadow: 0px 0px 16px rgba(0,0,0,0.3); float: left; }
figure, figure img, figcaption { width: 320px; height: 244px; box-sizing: border-box; }
figure img, figcaption { position: absolute; }
figcaption { background: #fff; text-align: center; padding-top: 6rem;     }
figure:hover { transform: rotateY(180deg);   }
```

The image-caption pairs are both exactly the same size, and positioned absolutely. Because the photographs come *after* the caption, they are displayed "on top" of the text. However, rotating each figure as a whole at this stage shows only the reverse side of the image, not the text.

Backface Visibility

Rotating elements around Z and Y axes brings up an interesting question: what happens when you rotate an element more than 180 degrees? What's on the other side of an image that had, until this moment, an effective "thickness" of 0?

Appearance in this state is determined by the backface-visibility property, which has a default value of visible. This means that when an element flips past 180, what is shown on the other side is the *reverse* of what's seen in the element's original orientation: images effectively become transparencies, equally visible on both sides, and text is rendered mirror-imaged. Turning backface-visibility to hidden causes the renderer to ignore the other side of the element when it rotates past 180 degrees; in most cases, this means less work for the renderer and, as a result, smoother, cleaner animations.

Transform Style

By default the browser will assume that children of a 3D transformed element take on the 3D transformations of their parent, but are projected onto the same plane: there is no "before" or "behind" sense for such child elements. Formally, this would be declared as transform-style: flat applied to the parent element.

If you wish child elements of a 3D-manipulated element to move in the same 3D space as their parents but be projected onto their own plane, a value of preserve-3d *must be applied to the parent element.* This allows you to place one child element behind the other, so that your card can have two visible "sides."

In this case there is one more addition to make to the code—together these properties will not, by themselves, be enough to provide the impression of a two-sided card. For the caption to be presented correctly on the other side of the image, it must be flipped horizontally *before* any animation takes place. (Think of two playing cards being placed back to back so that their faces are visible on either side).

Your code changes to what you can see in Listing 9-10.

Listing 9-10. Complete CSS Code for a More Complex 3D Gallery

```
body { background: hsl(100,0%,100%); font-family: Avenir, sans-serif; font-size: 1.5rem;
    margin-top: 400px; perspective: 1000px;      }
```

```
figure { margin: 20px; transition: 1s all linear;
    box-shadow: 0px 0px 16px rgba(0,0,0,0.3); float: left;
    transform-style: preserve-3d; }
figure, figure img, figcaption { width: 320px; height: 244px; box-sizing: border-box; }
figure img, figcaption { position: absolute; backface-visibility: hidden; }
figcaption { background: #fff; text-align: center; padding-top: 6rem;
    transform: rotateY(180deg);  }
figure:hover { transform: rotateY(180deg);  }
```

There's one more variation to consider: what if you want the other side of the photograph to be faintly visible through the caption? Turning off backface-visibility: hidden will not be enough to create this effect by itself. You will need to position each element in 3D space with a little more precision (see Listing 9-11).

Listing 9-11. Alternate Complete CSS Code for a More Complex 3D Gallery

```
body { background: hsl(100,0%,100%); font-family: Avenir, sans-serif; font-size: 1.5rem;
    margin-top: 400px; perspective: 1000px;      }
figure { margin: 20px; transition: 1s all linear;
    transform-style: preserve-3d; box-shadow: 0px 0px 16px rgba(0,0,0,0.3); float: left; }
figure, figure img, figcaption { width: 320px; height: 244px; box-sizing: border-box;   }
figure img, figcaption { position: absolute;  }
figcaption { background: #fff; text-align: center; padding-top: 6rem;
    transform: rotateY(180deg) translateZ(1px); opacity: 0.9;
}
figure:hover { transform: rotateY(180deg);  }
```

The very slight translation of the caption along the z-axis is enough to place the caption "behind" the image in such a way that the reversed aspect of the photograph underneath it can be seen, as shown in Figure 9-9.

Figure 9-9. *3D flipped image caption gallery with partially transparent reverse side*

A Circular 3D Gallery

You can take all of the photographs used so far and transform them into a fully circular 3D gallery that rotates on hover (Figure 9-10). The markup, shown in Listing 9-12, is very straightforward.

Figure 9-10. *An animated circular 3D gallery*

Listing 9-12. HTML Code for a Circular 3D Gallery

```
<div>
    <figure>
        <img src="färentuna-church.jpeg" alt="Färentuna church in Färingsö, Sweden">
        <img src="winter-trees.jpeg" alt="Trees in winter, Sweden">
        <img src="view-from-rastaholm.jpeg" alt="View From Rastaholm, Sweden">
        <img src="fall-park.jpeg" alt="Park in fall"> <img src="sunset2.jpeg" alt="Sunset">
        <img src="tulips2.jpeg" alt="Tulips">
        <img src="hepatica-nobilis.jpg" alt="Nepatica-nobilis">
        <img src="sunset.jpg" alt="Sunset">
        <img src="ekebyhosparken.jpg" alt="Ekebyhosparken">
    </figure>
</div>
```

You're going to push these images into a 3D circle by positioning them absolutely, so that they all stack on top of each other, locating their common transform-origin-z "back" in 3D space and rotating each independently around the Y axis. As there are eight images, each will be rotated in increments of 45 degrees to create an evenly distributed circle of photographs (Listing 9-13).

Listing 9-13. Basic CSS Code for a Circular 3D Gallery

```
div { perspective: 1000px; margin-top: 400px; width: 1400px; }
figure { transform-style: preserve-3d; height: 244px; transform-origin-x: 660px; }
img { width: 320px; height: 244px; position: absolute; left: 500px; }
figure, img { transform-origin-z: -500px; }
div img:nth-child(1) { transform: rotateY(0deg); }
div img:nth-child(2) { transform: rotateY(-45deg); }
div img:nth-child(3) { transform: rotateY(-90deg); }
div img:nth-child(4) { transform: rotateY(-135deg); }
div img:nth-child(5) { transform: rotateY(-180deg); }
div img:nth-child(6) { transform: rotateY(-225deg); }
div img:nth-child(7) { transform: rotateY(-270deg); }
div img:nth-child(8) { transform: rotateY(-315deg); }
```

Note that altering the height of the figure element changes the Y coordinate of the gallery origin, pitching the circle of images up and down in 3D space. At half the complete height of the images within it, the circle of photographs appears to be at "eye level" with the viewer.

Also note that you could use JavaScript to automate the distribution of the images—which you'll do in the next section.

There are two paths you could take to rotate the gallery on hover. One is to increase the rotateY value of each individual image by the same amount: an overly complex approach without resorting to scripting. As you can see, you've already set the images and the figure that surrounds them to have the same z origin, so your second option is to animate the figure itself (Listing 9-14).

Listing 9-14. CSS Animation Code for a Circular 3D Gallery

```
@keyframes spin { 100% { transform: rotateY(360deg); } }
figure:hover  { animation: spin 12s linear infinite; }
```

While the 3D and animation effects work well, the gallery is lacking one other aspect of realism: in real life, distant objects are not just smaller, they are also dimmer. Hiding the backfaces of the images won't work: that will make the images disappear, not fade, and adding spans behind each image, per the solution for the first gallery, is too much extra markup. Neither does the blur filter work on the pixel values of 3d-transformed images, at least not as of this writing.

There are a few possible ways of achieving the effect: the fourth and sixth images that can be seen at the "back" of the gallery circle could be dynamically set with opacity and made solid as they come to the forefront. Alternatively, a box-shadow applied equally to all sides of each image with no blur could be applied (Listing 9-15).

Listing 9-15. CSS Shading Effect for a Circular 3D Gallery

```
img { box-shadow: 0px 0px 0px 48px rgba(0,0,0,0.8); }
```

The limitation of this approach is that the background-color of the figure containing div or the body itself must be solid black; anything lighter will show the edges of the shadows. (See Figure 9-11).

Figure 9-11. A Circular 3D Gallery with Shading Effects

As each image remains effectively independent as its own element, you could combine the caption techniques explored in Chapter 3 with the photographs in the circular gallery, albeit with some changes to the markup (see Listing 9-16).

Listing 9-16. Code for a Circular 3D Image Gallery with Popup Captions

```
<style>
@keyframes spin {
    100% { transform: rotateY(360deg); }
}

body {  background: black; font-family: Georgia, serif; font-style: italic; font-size: 1.2rem; }
div#gallery { perspective: 1000px; margin-top: 400px; width: 1400px; }
div#inner{ transform-style: preserve-3d;
    transform-origin-x: 660px; transform-origin-z: -500px; height: 244px; }
figure, img { width: 320px; height: 244px; }
figure { left: 500px; position: absolute;  overflow: hidden; transform-origin-z: -500px; }
figcaption { background: hsla(0,0%,0%,0.5); color: #fff; position: relative; top: 0; padding:
8px;
    transition: 0.6s top linear; }
figure:hover figcaption { top: -38px; }

div#gallery:hover div#inner { animation: spin 24s linear infinite; }
div#gallery figure:nth-child(1) { transform: rotateY(0deg); }
div#gallery figure:nth-child(2) { transform: rotateY(-45deg);  }
div#gallery figure:nth-child(3) { transform: rotateY(-90deg); }
div#gallery figure:nth-child(4) { transform: rotateY(-135deg); }
div#gallery figure:nth-child(5) { transform: rotateY(-180deg); }
div#gallery figure:nth-child(6) { transform: rotateY(-225deg); }
div#gallery figure:nth-child(7) { transform: rotateY(-270deg); }
div#gallery figure:nth-child(8) { transform: rotateY(-315deg); }
</style>

<body>
<div id="gallery">
    <div id="inner">
    <figure>
        <img src="färentuna-church.jpeg" alt="Färentuna church in Färingsö, Sweden">
        <figcaption>Färentuna Church, Färingsö, Sweden</figcaption>
    </figure>
    <figure>
        <img src="winter-trees.jpeg" alt="Trees in winter, Sweden">
        <figcaption>Trees in winter, Sweden</figcaption>
     </figure>
    <figure>
        <img src="view-from-rastaholm.jpeg" alt="View From Rastaholm, Sweden">
        <figcaption>View From Rastaholm, Sweden</figcaption>
    </figure>
    <figure>
        <img src="fall-park.jpeg" alt="Park in fall">
        <figcaption>Swedish park in Fall</figcaption>
     </figure>
    <figure>
        <img src="sunset2.jpeg" alt="Sunset">
        <figcaption>Sunset</figcaption>
     </figure>
```

```
<figure>
    <img src="tulips2.jpeg" alt="Tulips">
    <figcaption>Tulips</figcaption>
</figure>
<figure>
    <img src="hepatica-nobilis.jpg" alt="Nepatica-nobilis">
    <figcaption>Nepatica nobilis</figcaption>
</figure>
<figure>
    <img src="sunset.jpg" alt="Sunset">
    <figcaption>Sunset</figcaption>
</figure>
<figure>
    <img src="ekebyhosparken.jpg" alt="Ekebyhosparken">
    <figcaption>Ekebyhosparken</figcaption>
</figure>
        </div>
    </div>
</body>
```

You can see a still of the result in Figure 9-12.

Figure 9-12. A circular 3D gallery with popup captions

Enhancing the Gallery with Level-4 Selectors and JavaScript

There are many ways to enhance the gallery you've created with JavaScript. The obvious and primary way is to take care of the initial rotation of the images with scripting rather than doing so by hand. (For the sake of simplicity, I'll assume that you have returned to the basic markup of the gallery shown in Listing 9-17).

Listing 9-17. JQuery Code to Automatically Distribute Images in a CSS3 Circular Gallery

```
<script>
var numberOfImgs = $("figure img").length;
var degreeSep = 360 / (numberOfImgs - 1);
var angle = 0;
for (i = 1; i < numberOfImgs; i++) {
```

```
    $("figure img:nth-child(" + (i) + ")").css('transform','rotateY('+ angle +'deg)');
    angle = angle + degreeSep;
}
</script>
```

This would eliminate eight repetitive lines of CSS and produce a far more flexible result: if images were added to or removed from within the figure, their distribution would be automatically adjusted. A more advanced version of the script might use basic trigonometry to determine that the size and number of the images and the origin-z distance were enough to provide acceptable spacing between photographs; if not, the image's width, height, and/or origin-z distance could be modified by JavaScript.

Second, you could allow the user to spin the gallery manually by detecting the mouse position inside the figure element and use its horizontal offset from the center to determine the amount of rotation for the gallery (Listing 9-18).

Listing 9-18. JQuery Code to Rotate a CSS3 Circular Gallery Based on Mouse Position

```
<script>
$("figure").mousemove(function(e) {
    var relativeX = e.pageX - (this.offsetLeft + 660);
    $(this).css('transform','rotateY('+ relativeX +'deg)');
});
</script>
```

This would mean removing the CSS3 animation and substituting in a transition, as shown in Listing 9-19.

Listing 9-19. CSS Code for JQuery Mouse-Position Rotation of a Circular Gallery

```
figure { transform-style: preserve-3d; transform-origin-x: 660px;
    transform-origin-z: -500px; height: 244px; transition: 2s transform linear; }
figure:hover { cursor: ew-resize; }
```

■ **Note** This could also be accomplished to some degree using pure CSS with two elements, each the height of the figure but half the width, placed left and right over the figure, with a hover pseudo-selector on each driving a clockwise and counterclockwise animation respectively. There are, however, two significant disadvantages: there could be no direct interactivity with the gallery underneath (i.e., no pop-up captions), as the two overlaid elements would capture all mouse events, and 2) using pure CSS would limit the animation to a set speed of rotation in either direction, as opposed to the further away = faster rotation of the JavaScript solution we looked at previously.

More advanced versions of this JavaScript—and versions more compatible with mobile UI conventions—might include a script to measure a mouse and/or fingertip drag movement on the screen, rotating the circular gallery a commensurate number of degrees. You could also add left-right buttons to rotate the gallery in increments.

Adding a CSS Level-4 Selector

Once it is supported by browsers, you could make the gallery more explorative by using the parent selector:

```
$figure img:nth-child(2):hover { transform: rotateY(-45deg); }
```

This would rotate the circular gallery as a whole to bring the current hovered image front and center.

3D CSS Transforms and Transitions for UI Elements

As a general rule, the requirement for clear navigation means that UI elements should employ as few visual "tricks" as possible. The following technique, derived from work pioneered by Hakim El Hattab (http://hakim.se, used with permission), uses the opposite approach: when the navigation is focused, the rest of the page is transitioned in 3D. A variation of the code is shown in Listing 9-20. You can see the results in Figure 9-13.

Figure 9-13. *Body content transformed with CSS3 with side-pull navigation*

Listing 9-20. HTML Code for Side-Pull Navigation

```
<!doctype html>
<html lang="en">
<head>
    <meta charset="utf-8">
    <title>3D fold-away menu</title>
    <link rel="stylesheet" href="wedge.css">
</head>
<body>
    <div class="meny">
    <h2>Other Demigods</h2>
    <ul>
        <li><a href="#">Aegir</a>
        <li><a href="#">Balder</a>
        <li><a href="#">Bragi</a>
        <li><a href="#">Eostra</a>
    </ul>
</div>
<div class="meny-arrow"> </div>
<div class="meny-contents">
    <div class="cover"></div>
    <article>
    <h1>Deigods of Asgard</h1>
    <p>HWÆT, WE GAR-DEna in geardagum, þeodcyninga þrym gefrunon.....
    </article>
```

```
</div>
</body>
<script src="meny.js"></script>
</html>
```

The attached stylesheet is shown in Listing 9-21.

Listing 9-21. CSS Stylesheet for Side-Pull Navigation

```
*{ margin: 0; padding: 0; }
html, body { height: 100%; overflow: hidden; }
body { background-color: #222;  font-family: Lato, Helvetica, sans-serif;
    font-size: 16px; color: #222; }
.meny-wrapper {perspective: 800; perspective-origin: 0% 50%; }
.meny, .meny-contents { box-sizing: border-box; transition: transform .5s ease;
    transform-origin: 0% 50%; }
.meny { display: none; position: fixed; height: 100%; width: 300px;
    z-index: 1; margin: 0px; padding: 20px;
    transform: rotateY( -30deg ) translateX( -97% ); }
.meny-ready .meny { display: block; }
.meny-active .meny { transform: rotateY( 0deg ); }
.meny-contents { background: #eee; padding: 20px 40px; width: 100%; height: 100%;
    overflow-y: auto; }
.meny-active .meny-contents { transform: translateX( 300px ) rotateY( 15deg ); }
.meny-contents .cover { display: none; position: absolute;
    width: 100%; height: 100%; top: 0; left: 0; visibility: hidden; z-index: 1000;
    opacity: 0;     background: linear-gradient(left,  rgba(0,0,0,0.15) 0%,rgba(0,0,0,0.65)
100%);
    transition: all .5s ease; }
.meny-ready .meny-contents .cover { display: block; }
.meny-active .meny-contents .cover { visibility: visible; opacity: 1; }
.meny-arrow { position: absolute; top: 45%; left: 12px; z-index: 10;
    font-family: sans-serif; font-size: 20px; color: #333;
    transition: left 0.8s cubic-bezier(0.680, -0.550, 0.265, 1.550); }
.meny-active .meny-arrow { left: -40px; opacity: 0; }
.meny-fold .meny, .meny-fold .meny-contents {transition: transform 0.6s ease; }
.meny-fold .meny-contents { position: fixed; z-index: 3; }
.meny-fold .meny {transform-origin: 50% 50%; }
.meny-fold .meny.right .cover { position: absolute;
    width: 100%; height: 100%; left: 0; top: 0; opacity: 1;
    background: linear-gradient(to right,  rgba(0,0,0,1) 0%,rgba(0,0,0,0) 90%); }
.meny-ready .meny-fold .meny.right .cover { transition: opacity 0.6s ease; }
.meny-active .meny-fold .meny.right .cover { opacity: 0; }
.meny-fold .meny.left { clip: rect( 0px, 150px, 10000px, 0px );
    transform: translate3d( -150px, 0, -300px ) rotateY( 90deg ) scale(1.25); }
.meny-active .meny-fold .meny.left { clip: initial; }
.meny-fold .meny.right { clip: rect( 0px, 300px, 10000px, 150px );
    transform: translate3d( -150px, 0, -300px ) rotateY( -90deg ) scale(1.25); }
.meny-active .meny-fold .meny.left, .meny-active .meny-fold .meny.right {
    transform: rotateY( 0deg ); }
a { color: #c2575b; text-decoration: none; transition: 0.15s color ease; }
a:hover { color: #f76f76; }
```

```
h1 { font-size: 24px; }
.meny { background: #333; color: #eee; }
.meny ul { margin-top: 10px; }
.meny ul li { list-style: none; font-size: 20px; padding: 3px 10px; }
.meny ul li:before { content: '-'; margin-right: 5px;
    color: rgba( 255, 255, 255, 0.2 ); }
.meny-contents>article { max-width: 400px; }
.meny-contents p { margin: 10px 0 10px 0; font-size: 16px; line-height: 1.32; }
```

Finally, the JavaScript,that covers hover, touch, and slide events is shown in Listing 9-22.

Listing 9-22. JavaScript for Side-Pull Navigation

```
(function(){
    var meny = document.querySelector( '.meny' );
    if (!meny || !meny.parentNode ) { return; }
    var menyWrapper = meny.parentNode;
    menyWrapper.className += ' meny-wrapper';
    var indentX = menyWrapper.offsetLeft,
    activateX = 40,
    deactivateX = meny.offsetWidth || 300,
    touchStartX = null,
    touchMoveX = null,
    isActive = false,
    isMouseDown = false;
    document.addEventListener( 'mousedown', onMouseDown, false );
    document.addEventListener( 'mouseup', onMouseUp, false );
    document.addEventListener( 'mousemove', onMouseMove, false );
    document.addEventListener( 'touchstart', onTouchStart, false );
    document.addEventListener( 'touchend', onTouchEnd, false );
    window.addEventListener( 'hashchange', onHashChange, false );
    onHashChange();
    document.documentElement.className += ' meny-ready';
    function onMouseDown( event ) { isMouseDown = true; }
    function onMouseMove( event ) {
        if( !isMouseDown ) { var x = event.clientX - indentX;
        if (deactivateX ) { deactivate(); }else if( x < activateX ) {activate(); } }
}
    function onMouseUp( event ) { isMouseDown = false; }
    function onTouchStart( event ) { touchStartX = event.touches[0].clientX - indentX;
    touchMoveX = null;
    if (isActive || touchStartX < activateX ) {
        document.addEventListener( 'touchmove', onTouchMove, false ); }
    }
function onTouchMove( event ) {
    touchMoveX = event.touches[0].clientX - indentX;
    if ( isActive && touchMoveX < touchStartX - activateX ) {
        deactivate(); event.preventDefault();
    }else if ( touchStartX < activateX && touchMoveX > touchStartX + activateX ) {
        activate();
        event.preventDefault(); } }
function onTouchEnd( event ) {
```

```
        document.addEventListener( 'touchmove', onTouchMove, false );
        if (touchMoveX === null ) {
            if (touchStartX > deactivateX ) { deactivate(); }
            else if (touchStartX < activateX * 2) { activate(); }}}

function onHashChange( event ) {
    if( window.location.hash.match( 'fold' ) && !document.body.className.match( 'meny-fold' ) ) {
        addClass( document.body, 'meny-fold' );
        var clone = document.createElement( 'div' );
        clone.className = 'meny right';
clone.innerHTML = meny.innerHTML + '<div class="cover"></div>';
document.body.appendChild( clone );
addClass( meny, 'left' );
        } else {
removeClass( document.body, 'meny-fold' );
var clone = document.querySelector( '.meny.right' );
if (clone ) {
    clone.parentNode.removeChild( clone ); } } }

function activate() { if (isActive === false ) {
    isActive = true;
    addClass( document.documentElement, 'meny-active' ); }}

function deactivate() {
    if( isActive === true ) {
    isActive = false;
    removeClass( document.documentElement, 'meny-active' ); }
}

function addClass( element, name ) {
    element.className = element.className.replace( /\s+$/gi, '' ) + ' ' + name;          }

function removeClass( element, name ) {
    element.className = element.className.replace( name, '' );
}
})();
```

Brought together, the HTML, JavaScript, and CSS create the effect you see in Figure 9-10 for desktop browsers and mobile devices.

Summary

3D transforms, transitions, and animations can be used to add depth and perspective to your web content. While it can be difficult to visualize the z axis in the context of a flat 2D screen, use of the principles discussed here and in previous chapters—including manipulation of the origin and transformation around a point, use of forced perspective, backface visibility, and transform style—can help a lot.

So far, you've been producing all your code by hand. While that's the best way to learn, CSS code generation can be made much quicker and more efficient with well-configured tools, for which you will find recommendations in the next chapter. You'll also take a look at where the next innovations in CSS, together with related technologies, are likely to come from.

■ ■ ■

CHAPTER 10

Tools, Technologies, and the Future of CSS Animation

As a set of W3C modules that are only beginning to move from Working Draft to Candidate Recommendation status, the CSS Transforms, Transitions, and Animation specifications do not yet have the robust industry toolset that older, finalized specs boast. Software developers can't be blamed for the relative paucity of tools: the specification has been a moving target, making application development challenging. At the same time, the W3C is moving forward on new technologies, making tool development even harder, while CSS itself becomes much more powerful.

Despite the rapid pace of change, there are a number of solutions available to speed and streamline workflow and development in CSS3 animations, both for backward compatibility in older browsers and forward-looking applications for development now and in the future. Before we get to that, however, you should take a moment to appreciate how to effectively use the skills you've learned so far.

Writing Effective CSS3 Animations and Transitions: Avoiding Reflows

There are two actions in CSS that are computationally expensive for a browser to handle: repaints and reflows.

A page *reflow* is initiated when the layout of page content is altered: think of the appearance of a fluid site changing as the browser window narrows. A *repaint* occurs when an element changes its visibility, but in ways that do not affect the layout of its neighbors: when an element's visibility, opacity, or background color changes, for example.

Of the two, reflows are usually the more detrimental to performance, as a reflow will "ripple" through the DOM tree from the affected element downwards through all child nodes and those after, forcing multiple elements to change their position. In many cases, reflows can essentially redraw the entire page. Reflow actions may not be significant to performance on modern desktop machines, but can be a critical hit on lesser-powered devices, such as smartphones. Most relevant to our interests, use of any pseudoelement, such as :hover, or a script manipulating the DOM, will initiate a reflow.

■ **Note** If you're more of a visually-oriented person, you can see a very slowed-down reflow process in Firefox as it lays out the google.co.jp homepage for the first time on YouTube at www.youtube.com/watch?v=nJtBUHyNBxs.

While browser reflows are unavoidable, their impact can be minimized and localized by following a few rules:

- *Try to affect the element you wish to style directly, rather than its parent.* That is, try to limit the scope of any reflow: rather than altering the class of a container element to affect its children, try to affect the children themselves directly. This does not avoid all reflows—altering the height of an element may affect the dimensions of its parent, for example, causing a reflow to ripple up—but it is a good general rule.

- *Avoid setting inline styles.* Most especially, avoid the creation of multiple inline styles. Instead, externalize the relevant CSS into a class and then change the class. A work process that emphasizes the opposite—trying to manipulate an inline style, or merging styles between embedded, linked, and inline styles, for example—will likely cause multiple reflows as each is adjusted.

- *Apply animations to elements using* transform, *or to elements that are positioned absolutely or fixed.* Elements with these characteristics do not affect the position of others, meaning that only the affected element will be repainted, without the cost of a reflow.

- *Create animations that are "internal" to an element with a fixed height and width and/or that has* overflow:hidden *applied.* Animations inside such elements will not affect others, avoiding opportunities for reflows.

- *Specify set image dimensions.* If the browser knows the width and height of image elements, it will not have to push content around as the image is placed on the page. Obviously this is complicated by current trends in responsive design.

- *Avoid long descendant selectors.* Long descendant selectors with many tags tend to be computationally expensive.

- *Avoid use of the universal selector.* The wildcard (*) selector is the most computationally burdensome selector of all.

- *Try to specify the property you wish to transition, rather than using "all".* While not directly related to reflows, using the "all" option in a transition is wasteful, as the browser is then forced to track *every* possible change to the element. Specifying a single property you wish to track and change, such as opacity, is far more efficient.

- *Use a style profiler.* (See Figure 10-1.)

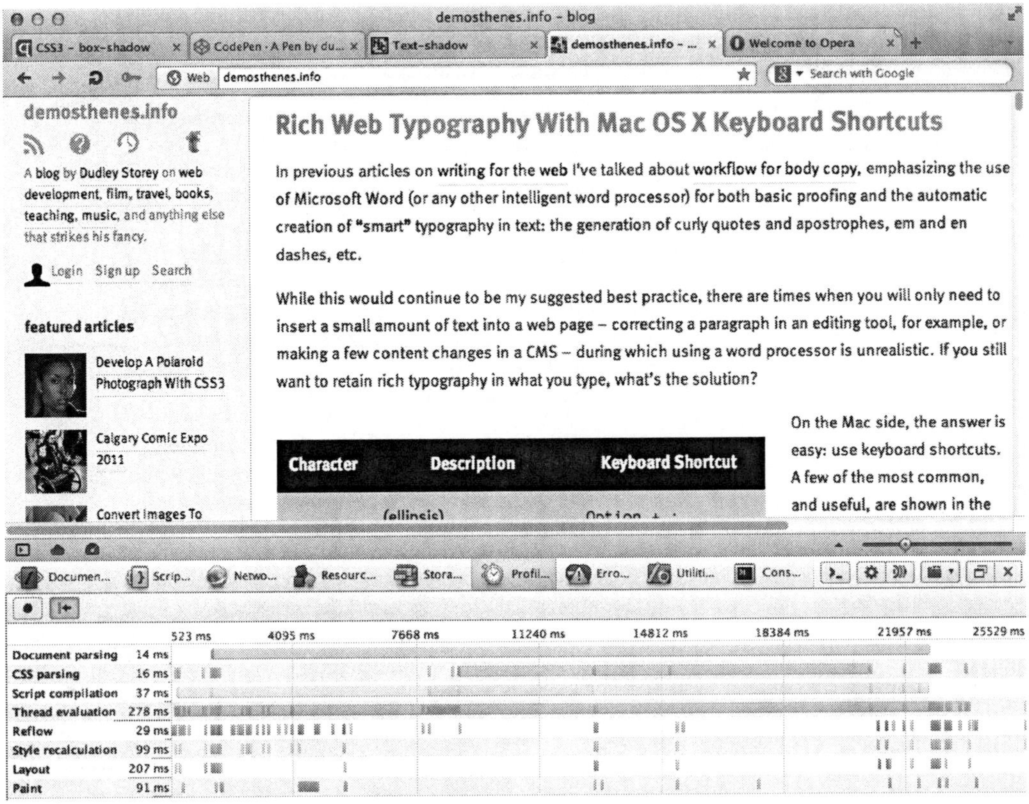

Figure 10-1. *A profile tool, such as the Timeline Developer Tool in Chrome or the Style Profiler in Opera Dragonfly, can help to highlight areas in which your CSS is particularly inefficient or slow*

Automatic Prefixing Tools: Client-Side

In order to gain support in older browser versions, CSS3 Transforms, Transitions, and Animations must be written as separate declarations with the correct browser vendor prefixes, as discussed in Chapter 1. While maintaining five different lines of code for a single transition is certainly achievable, maintaining anything more complex can be a nightmare. While tools such as Prefixr (http://prefixr.com) can add prefixes to existing code, they're not realistic options for code that is open to change: any alterations to the original CSS means you will need to go through the same process again to add prefixes. There are several possible solutions to this issue, one server-side, the other client-side, each with its own advantages and disadvantages.

-prefix-free

Greek developer Lea Verou (http://lea.verou.me) has written a popular, lightweight, and effective script that, dropped into a page, will customize any non-prefixed CSS code as needed for the browser that is viewing the page (http://leaverou.github.com/prefixfree/).

This is my personal preferred solution for lightweight work (such as making a CSS3 animation in the header of a blog post); it allows me to write single lines of code that follow the expected final spec, minimizing file size, and it lets the script handle backward compatibility. There are a few issues to be aware of, however:

- There is a strong argument to be made that this kind of CSS declaration transformation is not the role of a client-side script, but a server-side one, as discussed below.

- Users who browse a site that uses the -prefix-free script but who have JavaScript turned off—either directly or through a browser extension such as NoScript (http://noscript.net)—*and* are using a browser that is still dependent on vendor prefixes will not see any transforms, transitions, or animations. However, this particular audience is small and—especially in regard to the number of browsers moving to support non-prefixed CSS3—rapidly diminishing in size. In addition, if you've followed the principles of progressive enhancement and graceful degradation in Chapter 2, the lack of CSS3 should not affect a user's ability to enjoy or use your site.

- The delivery of standard prefixed CSS3 from the server may be slightly faster in some cases, due to the fact that -prefix-free must process the CSS client-side before it can be used. In practice, this is usually balanced out by the server-side processing required in other solutions, or the larger file size associated with fully-prefixed CSS code.

- Unprefixed properties that appear in inline styles won't be transformed by -prefix-free for Firefox 3.6 or lower (a very unusual case, at least for most sites and their visitors).

SASS, LESS, Compass and Codekit

SASS (http://sass-lang.com) and LESS (http://lesscss.org) are perhaps best described as "meta frameworks" for CSS, allowing features such as variables, functions, loops, automatic validation, optimization, and minification of code, nested rules, and (the most relevant to our interests here) automatic prefixing of CSS3 through "mixins." Both frameworks promote themselves as *CSS Extensions*, although this should not be considered an endorsement by the W3C. (That being said, many of the innovations CSS frameworks have promoted, such as variables, are being taken on in new CSS modules.)

LESS works through JavaScript, "translating" a LESS-infused stylesheet (styles.less) into browser-ready CSS at runtime: as a result, it shares many of the advantages (and disadvantages) of -prefix-free. SASS takes the approach of precompiling stylesheets written in SASS (styles.scss) into a complete .css file that can be used by every browser.

Compass (http://compass-style.org/) bundles many of the best additions for SASS together. Managing different SASS tools and extensions is made somewhat difficult by the fact they they must be controlled through the command line as Ruby gems. CodeKit (http://incident57.com/codekit) is a framework manager for Mac OS X that pulls them all together (including LESS, Stylus, and Compass) in a graphical user interface and some other nice features—such as automatically refreshing the page in an open browser when the CSS has changed.

Finally, including a "mixin" helps shortcut your code still further; a library collection of scripts such as Bourbon (http://thoughtbot.com/bourbon/) or Compass will allow you to type a simple transition in SASS in this way. (The code in Listing 10-1 is shown in Compass syntax.)

Listing 10-1. Using a SASS Mixin to Generate Vendor-Prefixed Code

```
#element {
@include transition-property(width);
@include transition-duration(2s);
@include transition-timing-function(ease-in); }

#element:hover {
  width: 180%
}
```

The code in Listing 10-4 will be automatically expanded to cover all browser vendor prefixes when the code is compiled.

Automatic Prefixing Tools: Server-Side

CSS Prefixer (http://cssprefixer.appspot.com) takes a server-side approach: operating as a Python script, it converts nonprefixed CSS into vendor declarations when a .css file is served. While it is more dependable than a client-side solution like -prefix-free or LESS, it does not attempt any kind of client detection: the CSS produced is prefixed for every possible browser, significantly expanding the codebase and file size.

GUI-Based CSS3 Animation Tools

Text editors start to become challenged as CSS3 animations grow more ambitious and complex: while they are perfectly suited for small projects, visual tools have significant advantages when it comes to animating multiple elements separately. The field is growing rapidly and the following is merely a selection.

Sencha Animator

One of the first popular tools on the block, Sencha Animator (www.sencha.com/products/animator) uses the familiar timeline UI together with a complete suite of transform and keyframing tools to create CSS animations (see Figure 10-2).

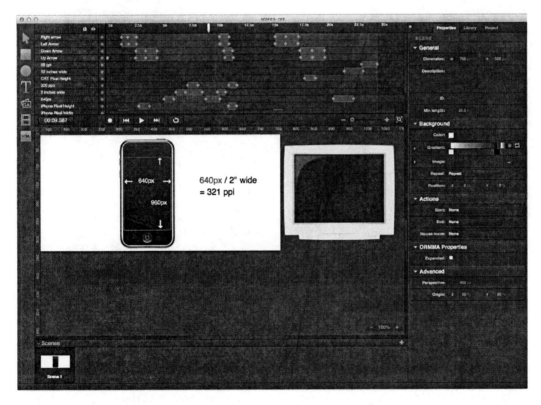

Figure 10-2. *Screenshot of Sencha Animator*

The application's output is somewhat obfuscated, however, making the result difficult to work with in any other application; its default means of presenting the work (via JavaScript, and solely using vendor-prefixed code for Firefox and Webkit) means that the result must be heavily edited for full cross-browser compatibility.

Adobe Edge Animate

The newest addition to the range of CSS animation tools (and barely out of beta), Adobe Edge Animate (http://html.adobe.com/edge/animate) is a very promising application that builds on the standard Adobe UI (and the default dark-gray theme of Adobe's Creative Suite 6, as shown in Figure 10-3) but which adds a number of significant improvements. It also uses JavaScript as a framework to support CSS3 animations, but does so in a way that supports all modern browsers and older versions with vendor prefixes.

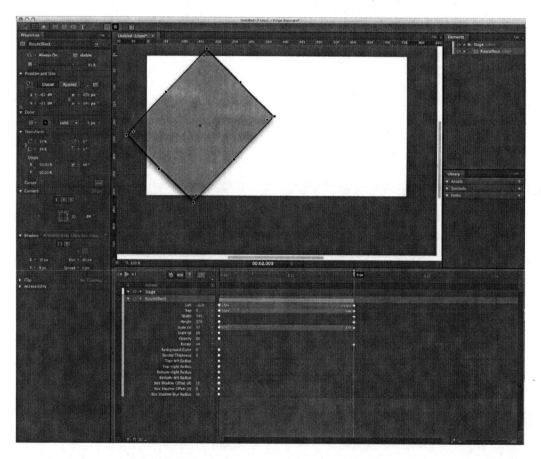

Figure 10-3. Screenshot of Adobe Edge Animate

Animatable

After making a splash by creating a very popular CSS3 animation for the opening credits of AMC television's *Mad Men* (see http://stuffandnonsense.co.uk/content/demo/madmanimation/ and Figure 10-4), development of Animatable (http://animatable.com) appears to have stalled, or at least gone quiet; it's still worth keeping an eye on the product for breaking changes, however.

Figure 10-4. *Still from the Mad Men credit sequence CSS animation created by Animatable*

Tumult Hype

Another web animation GUI, of all of the tools described here Tumult Hype is the most heavily invested in JavaScript: the application describes itself as an "HTML5 animation tool" rather than a CSS3 development program. This is a pity, since its UI is probably the most intuitive to use, as shown in Figure 10-5.

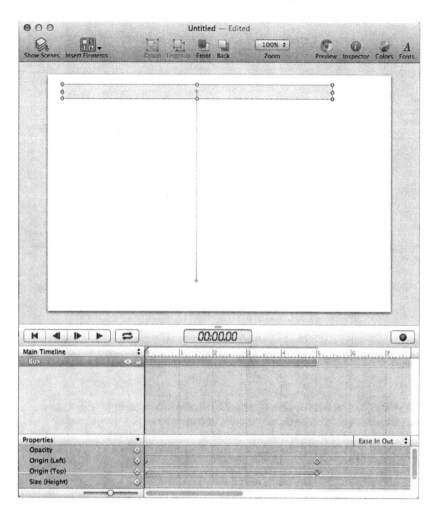

Figure 10-5. *Screenshot of Tumult Hype animation UI*

Future Trends: CSS Custom Filters

An Adobe technology previously known as Web Shaders, the W3C has adopted this new technology as a proposal named CSS Custom Filters.

The standard filters explored in Chapter 9 might be best described as simple image converters: hue-rotate, blur, and sepia consistently shift all the pixels of the affected image, but nothing more. Standard CSS Filters cannot affect individual pixels: you can't use a filter on half an image, nor can you use a filter to distort an image. Custom Filters explicitly splits this process into two separate functions: programmable *fragment shaders* can be used to adjust the color of pixels, animate wipes, and create custom transitions; *vertex shaders* treat the area of every DOM element as a visual mesh, allowing the designer to ripple, bend, twist, and distort the surface of images as well as every other element.

A call to a custom filter, as proposed in the current specification, looks like Listing 10-2.

Listing 10-2. A Transition Utilizing a CSS Custom Filter

```
#shaded-element {
filter: custom(url('wobble.vs')
      40 40,
      amplitude 60,
      amount 0.0);
)
transition: filter ease-in-out 2s;
}
```

The number pair 40 40 works to define the density of the virtual mesh that the element is divided into: more divisions will create a smoother, more fluid, and detailed effect. amplitude is the strength of the effect, and amount is the degree to which the element is affected.

The wobble.vs (vertex shader) file referred to in the first line is written in the OpenGL ES shading language, utilizing the same syntax used in WebGL to create browser-native 3D on web pages, as shown in Listing 10-3.

Listing 10-3. An OpenGL ES Shader

```
precision mediump float;
attribute vec3 a_position;
attribute vec2 a_texCoord;
uniform mat4 u_projectionMatrix;
uniform float amplitude;
uniform float amount;
varying vec2 v_texCoord;
const float rotate = 20.0;
const float PI = 3.1415926;
mat4 rotateX(float a) {...}
mat4 rotateY(float a) {...}
mat4 rotateZ(float a) {...}
void main() {
    v_texCoord = a_texCoord.xy;
    vec4 pos = vec4(a_position, 1.0);
    float r = 1.0 - abs((amount - 0.5) / 0.5);
    float a = r * rotate * PI / 180.0;
    mat4 rotX = rotateX(a);
    mat4 rotY = rotateY(a / 4.0);
    mat4 rotZ = rotateZ(a / 8.0);
    float dx = 0.01 * cos(3.0 * PI * (pos.x + amount)) * r;
    float dy = 0.01 * cos(3.0 * PI * (pos.y + amount)) * r;
    float dz = 0.1 * cos(3.0 * PI * (pos.x + pos.y + amount)) * r;
    pos.x += dx;
    pos.y += dy;
    pos.z += dz;
    gl_Position = u_projectionMatrix * rotZ * rotY * rotX * pos;
}
```

As you can see, this is *very* different from the CSS you are familiar with: it is an entirely new language. Yet applying all this as a transition for the #shaded-element (shown in Listing 10-4) very much returns to the principles you explored in Chapter 2.

Listing 10-4. A Transition Utilizing a CSS Custom Filter

```
#shaded-element:hover {
    filter: custom(url('wobble.vs')
    40 40,
    amplitude 60,
    amount 1.0);
}
```

All of the controls on the filter remain the same, except for the amount; the transition on the original default state will ensure that the element transitions smoothly into the new hover state.

Custom Filters promise an extreme degree of visual control over HTML content that is unachievable with standard CSS, and that has the potential to revolutionize both animation and interaction on the web. However, that process will take some time: the specification is very new and, as of this writing, is only supported in very recent builds of Chrome. Finalizing the specification, gaining cross-browser support, and dealing with important issues such as security is likely to take several years.

Future Trends: Blending and Compositing

Adobe is also advancing CSS in the area of blending and compositing, taking the controls you might be familiar with in Adobe PhotoShop and Illustrator—such as multiply, darken, lighten, and advanced clipping—and translating them to CSS.

While this work is only at the proposal stage, it promises a far more visually vibrant web if implemented, especially if the properties can be animated. It is conceivable that in the long term, bitmap and vector illustration tools will increasingly become content *creators* in the early stages of the production process, while a majority of editing work will be done live in the browser using CSS.

Future Trends: Reconciling CSS3 and SVG

For two web technologies that can work so well together and have influenced each other so powerfully (particularly in the area of transforms and filters), CSS and SVG continue to have a remarkable number of conflicts.

While CSS can be used to animate a number of SVG presentation attributes as well as SVG images themselves (as you saw in Chapter 9), and while SVG can animate itself—using the <animate> tag, part of a standard known as SMIL (Synchronized Multimedia Integration Language)—merging the two is currently extremely difficult. CSS Keyframe Animation rules override CSS Transitions and SVG (SMIL) Animations, but are conflicted when it comes to CSS Transitions and SMIL Animations. The question of compatibility is complicated further by Internet Explorer 10's lack of support for SMIL.

These issues are being addressed by the W3C CSS-SVG Effects Task Force (www.w3.org/Graphics/fx), but the developments and changes that may come out of that process are unknown at this time.

Summary

Web animation technologies have come a very long way from the days when Flash and JavaScript were the only ways to achieve motion on a web page, and they are sure to go further still, with the tools and syntaxes you have looked at here—and with those yet to come.

This book has offered both an introduction to and a deep dive into modern standards-based CSS3 animation. Along the way, you've explored CSS Transforms, Transitions, keyframe Animations, and 3D manipulations, and coupled them with other technologies and techniques such as SVG, JavaScript, and responsive design. Supportive tools for developing with this mélange of languages are coming along, but the most reliable—and the only one that will allow you the freedom to remain at the cutting edge, should you choose to pursue it—is the humble text editor.

The prolonged period of writing long cross-browser compatibility CSS declarations with vendor prefixes is coming to a close. Most recent browser versions are dropping them entirely for the properties you've looked at in this book.

The new environment that this rapid adoption of technologies is forming—the "Next Web"—promises to be more open, richer in possibility, and more creative than anything that has come become. I'm excited to see what new vistas it may uncover, as I hope you are too.

I look forward to seeing your work and getting your feedback—and being inspired in turn by your explorations and innovations in CSS3 animation.

Index

■ H

Horizontal drop-down navigation, 69
Horizontal navigation interfaces, 58

■ I, J, K, L, M, N, O

Image card stack, 40
   Css transforms, 42
   offset origin, 43
   transform origin, 42
Image fan reveal, 40
   card fan gallery, 44
   foreground, 45
   hinted card fan, 44
   HTML and CSS code, 46
   src attribute, 45
Image gallery
   adding captions, 36
   HTML markup, 34
   improving gallery, 35
   initial CSS, 35
   initiating event
      active, 36
      target, 37

■ P, Q

Page reflow, 155
Popup image, 37
   Animated image, 38
   CSS
      hide, 40
      transition, 40
   rem font size, 39

■ R, S

Responsive Web Design (RWD), 117
   without transitions, 118, 120

background image, 120
   image in minimum and maximum, 120
   resize image and video, 118
  with transitions, 121
ripple, 155

■ T

Transformation, CSS, 9
   description, 9
   DOM, 11
   merging, 17
   rotation transformation, 10–11
      description, 10
      floating an image, 11
      possible unit systems, 11
   scale transform, 14
   skew, 16
   translate modifier, 16
   webkit CSS3 transform aliasing issue, 13
Transitions, CSS, 18
   delaying and combining effects, 21–23
      description, 21
      easing functions, 22
      properties, 21
      transition timing functions, 23
   description, 18
   timing, 19
Tweening process, 75

■ U, V

UI button depress transition, 66
UI button reveal transition, 67

■ W, X, Y, Z

World Wide Web Consortium (W3C), 1

CPSIA information can be obtained at www.ICGtesting.com
Printed in the USA
LVOW091711111212

311165LV00003B/8/P